CAVING

CAVING

Steven Boga

STACKPOLE
BOOKS

Published by
STACKPOLE BOOKS
5067 Ritter Road
Mechanicsburg, PA 17055

Printed in the United States

10 9 8 7 6 5 4 3 2 1

First edition

Photography by Dave Bunnell

Illustrations by Thom Aubrey/The River Studio and Caroline Stover

My Friend, The Carbide Lamp reprinted in the 1993 edition of *Speleo Digest*. Used with permission of the National Speleological Society.

Library of Congress Cataloging-in-Publication Data

Boga, Steve, 1947-
 Caving / by Steven Boga
   p.   cm.
  ISBN 0-8117-2710-6(pb)
  1. Caving   I. Title
GV200.62.B64
796.52'5—dc21   199796-29881
                                                                              CIP

To Floyd Collins, who died for our sins.

CONTENTS

ACKNOWLEDGEMENTS

Besides the usual acknowledgements—my editors Mark Allison and Dave Richwine, my wife Karen, my parents for showing me my first cave—I'd like to thank the National Speleological Society for contributing advice and resource material for this book.

My deepest gratitude is reserved for David Bunnell, editor of the NSS newsletter and caver-photographer extraordinaire, for his editorial input and gorgeous subterranean shots that decorate this book.

INTRODUCTION

Unless you grew up in cave country with a passion for subterranean retreats, your reaction to caves may depend upon your first literary contact with them. If your familiarity with caves derives from *Alice in Wonderland*, for example, you may have mixed feelings. The Cheshire Cat was fun, but the Queen of Hearts was unsettling. Recalling *Ali Baba and the Forty Thieves*, your reaction may be more positive. In this, the most popular tale from the collection known as the *Arabian Nights*, thieves stash their stolen treasure in a secret cave, and Ali Baba sees them do it. He learns their secret password, "Open Sesame," which he uses to enter the cave and make off with the gold himself. If, on the other hand, your first contact was in Greek mythology, caves may conjure up frightening visions of the Minotaur, a monster with the head of a bull and the body of a human. Or perhaps you recall Tom Sawyer being pursued through an underground labyrinth, and you break out in a cold sweat whenever *cave* comes up in a crossword puzzle.

A recent poll ranked the things people fear most:
1. Speaking before a group
2. Heights
3. Insects and bugs
4. Financial problems
5. Deep water
6. Sickness
7. Death
8. Flying
9. Loneliness
10. Dogs
11. Driving or riding in a car
12. Darkness

Although caves offer a great escape from dogs, cars, public speaking, and financial problems, an underground excursion may force you to confront darkness, loneliness, and insects, and possibly heights or deep water. Be prepared.

If you have gotten past the fears and developed an active interest in caving, a good starting point would be to visit some commercial caves. With their electric lights and stairs (maybe even elevators), they are decidedly tame compared with undeveloped caves; the drawback is that such routine descents probably won't tell you a lot about your visceral response to being underground.

The next step would be to seek out capable cavers who are willing to lead you through caves appropriate for novices. The best way to find such people is through the National Speleological Society in Huntsville, Alabama. Membership in the society is open to anyone interested in caves, which includes cave scientists and owners, conservationists, adventurers, and people who simply enjoy visiting and exploring caves. The NSS is subdivided into local caving chapters, called grottos. Check the Resources chapter at the end of this book for the grotto nearest you.

Lest you think that caving is nothing more than a series of slogs through cramped, muddy crawlways, consider the subterranean career of David Bunnell, editor of the National Speleological Society's periodical, the *NSS News.*

He grew up in Delaware, where caves are about as common as icebergs. In his early teens, he and his family vacationed at Maine's Acadia National Park, where they heard about a sea cave called Anemone. David was so intrigued that he visited it every day.

At age sixteen, he entered his first limestone cave, Crystal Cave in California's Sequoia National Park. Although fascinated, he put caving on hold until he was in college. Then, while attending the University of Delaware, he joined an outdoor club. "I was a rock climber," he says, "but there was a caving contingent that kind of drew me in."

In 1973 he crawled through his first muddy hole, a nondescript cave in Pennsylvania. "There were no formations or anything particularly redeeming about that cave," he notes, "but I was taken by the totally different world down there. I began going caving every weekend."

When it came time to choose a graduate school, he applied only to colleges within striking distance of caves, finally settling on the University of Virginia at Charlottesville. He caved extensively in Virginia and West Virginia, finding enough attractions to keep him busy every weekend for five years. In one Virginia cave, he found connections between various passages, eventually revealing a cave 50 miles long. "The high point was the discovery of a huge chamber about 250 feet high, with a 150-foot waterfall plunging into it," he says. He helped map another cave that the army had blown shut during World War II. It was thought to be a tiny, insignificant cave, but the efforts of David and others revealed a cave 3 miles long, replete with pristine speleothems.

In 1980 he moved to California, stepping up the adventure level significantly. Highlights included caving in the Grand Canyon after packing in for 15 miles and mapping New Mexico's Lechuguilla Cave. Originally believed to be nothing more than a pit, Lechuguilla is now known to be 90 miles long. "Lechuguilla has the most outrageous crystal formations in the world," he says unequivocally. "Things that aren't found anyplace else. Probably my greatest caving moment occurred there. We discovered a huge chamber, maybe 200 feet across, with a giant bathtub ring around it. At the bottom was a deep blue-green lake, surrounded on all sides with a red, doilylike shelfstone. As we peered into its depths, we saw stalagmites growing underwater. Years later, I got to dive that lake with scuba gear."

His passion for caving and cave diving has taken him all over the world. He has cave-dived in Florida and Yucatán, discovered lava tubes in Hawaii, and gone project caving in Papua, New Guinea, and Borneo. Maybe the most memorable trip was a National Geographic expedition to Belize. "While mapping new caves, we found areas rich in Mayan artifacts. At one point we climbed way up some flowstone, on steps carved by the Maya. We were way up in this dome looking down at a river—beautiful! At the top we came upon a chamber filled with Mayan ollas, essentially big ceramic pots. It was staggering to think they were made a thousand years ago. One had been left

Caver rappelling by a waterfall,
Sistema Chichicasapan, Mexico

under dripping water, and there was a 3-foot stalagmite growing out of the middle of it. I took pictures of that."

He delighted in mapping newly discovered lava caves on the big island of Hawaii. It was there in 1994 that he had what he calls his "dream week." In a seven-day period, he and his team found what was, at 850 feet, the deepest lava pit in the United States, and then helped make a connection to complete the longest and deepest lava tube in the United States. "You can now drop into that lava tube, truck along for hours, and emerge 30 miles later, having dropped 2,900 vertical feet in the process."

Today Bunnell and many other veteran cavers are into project caving—subterranean exploration with a purpose. The goal may include mapping or finding connecting passages, but a love of cave exploration is always at the heart of it. A few years ago, Bunnell was shown Painted Cave in the Channel Islands off the coast of California. "It's believed to be the world's largest sea cave," he says. "You can take a boat 800 feet in, and I began to wonder just how big sea caves get. So I bought a boat and headed for the Channel Islands to find out."

After mapping all the caves of Santa Cruz Island, he wrote a book on it. Then he mapped and authored a book on the 135 sea caves of nearby Anacapa Island. Bunnell is also one of the leading cave photographers in the country, and his shots have appeared in magazines, in books, and on CD-ROMs.

The Science of Caves

Caves are cavities in rock, naturally occurring holes in the ground. They range from rock overhangs not much larger than a pool table to cave systems hundreds of miles long. Although shallow caves can be of great interest to archaeologists, they offer little to speleologists and will not be the focus here.

GEOLOGY

The vast majority of caves are hollowed out by the action of mildly acidic water dissolving limestone, although volcanic caves may develop as lava tubes and streams of meltwater may carve ice caves in glaciers. Limestone is impervious to water until it fractures, which it is prone to do. Slightly acidic water is able to penetrate those fractures and dissolve the limestone. That creates wider cracks that let in more water, dissolving still more limestone. The result, over tens of thousands of years or longer, can be majestic subterranean sculptures of mind-boggling beauty and complexity.

 The groundwater that dissolves limestone to form cave chambers contains carbon dioxide absorbed from vegetation, soil, and the atmosphere. Some carbon dioxide unites with the limestone to form calcium bicarbonate, which may be dissolved and carried in water flowing through the cave. When the water carrying the calcium bicarbonate evaporates, it releases the carbon dioxide, and what's left over is deposited as crystals of calcium carbonate (*calcite* or *aragonite*).

Large formations in Ogle Cave, New Mexico

Over time, large chambers and long passages may be etched out of the limestone. If the water table drops or the land rises, the water in these chambers or passages drains away, leaving them dry. If the water table rises and falls more than once, passages develop on several levels, as in Kentucky's expansive Mammoth Cave, which has at least five distinct levels.

If the surface above a cave collapses, a sinkhole develops. Sinkholes offer entryways for surface streams, animals, and even waste. When a cave's passages are intersected by streams cutting downward from the surface, the result is fairly horizontal access and, occasionally, huge, majestic openings up to 250 feet high. If the limestone beds become tilted, water may dissolve passages along fracture lines to great depths. The famed Pierre-St. Martin Cave in the French Pyrenees, for example, is more than 3,280 feet deep.

Speleothems

Imagine the joy you would feel stumbling upon a vast underground chamber decorated with stalactites, stalagmites, delicate flowerlike structures called helectites, and hardened flowstone crafted into terraces. Above you, thin, translucent sheets of calcite, called *drapery*, hang down 10 feet or more from the ceiling. They are formed by drops of water flowing down an inclined ceiling, leaving behind a sinuous trail of mineral matter. In some caves, draperies have sharp, serrated edges, called *fringes,* that resemble the teeth of a saw. If the water contains impurities, orange or brown streaks appear as the draperies develop, giving them a banded look not unlike fried bacon.

If the crystals remain in contact with the ceiling, they develop into a *stalactite,* a small, circular, hollow tube that may descend several feet toward the floor. Minerals such as copper or iron may color the stalactite. The most common, and certainly the most delicate, of these formations are called *soda straws.* These occur when seepage water deposits a thin ring of calcite around the circumference of the drop where it clings to the roof. The drop falls, another takes its place, and the thin calcite ring slowly grows into a hollow rock tube. Straws, though fragile, may exceed 10 feet in length if undisturbed. They are unique among cave formations in that they always have the same diameter—that of a water drop. When dozens of them form in proximity, they suggest an upside-down forest of knitting needles.

Tapering, or carrot, stalactites often start as straws, filling out when the central hole becomes blocked and water seeps down the sides of the straw. Soda straws and carrots, like nearly all stalactites, reach a water-drop point at their lower end.

Stalagmites, stumpier in appearance, are created when water drops directly to the cave floor and splashes outward, releasing carbon dioxide and leaving crystals that begin to grow upward with a rounded top and no central canal. Left undisturbed, they can become enormous, up to 33 feet tall and almost that big in diameter. The only limita-

Caver on sharp pinnacles, Borneo

tion on their height, other than human interference, is a junction with a stalactite or a cave roof. When that meeting takes place, a *column* is formed.

The rate of growth of stalactites and stalagmites is not constant, because it depends on water percolation from the surface. Although the average rate of growth is approximately .08 inch per year, there are too many variables involved to determine their age by simply measuring their length.

Cave Zones

Although people often think of caves as places of total darkness, scientists delineate three cave zones: entrance zone, twilight zone, and dark zone.

The *entrance zone* has most of the same environmental conditions as the surface. Animals have long sought refuge in entrance zones, and humans have used them for shelter and burial grounds since prehistoric times. Alabama's Russell Cave shows evidence of human habitation dating back nine thousand years. Unearthed in the Upper Cave at Zhoukoudian near Beijing (Peking) were stone tools and skeletal remains of *Homo sapiens* (modern humans) dating back about thirty thousand years.

The *twilight zone* is sheltered from direct sunlight and has a more moderate environment than its neighboring zones. It is home to a large, diverse population of animals, including salamanders, bats, and, during severe winters, bears. Some animals hibernate in the twilight zone, but most exit to feed.

The *dark zone,* the true cave environment, is as silent and dark as a tomb. It is an unusually stable region, with little wind, a relative humidity near 100 percent, and a relatively constant temperature. This environment could hardly seem less hospitable to life, yet astonishingly, some species thrive in the deep recesses of the earth—albeit with significant physical adaptations.

BIOLOGY

The dark zone of caves is home to a very specialized group of animals that have made unique adaptations, including bacteria, which require no light, and dozens of species of small fish, shrimp, sala-manders, crayfish, beetles, millipedes, and spiders. These animals—collectively known as *troglobites* (cave dwellers)—creep and crawl, slither and scuttle, swim and fly, yet for the most part they thrive unseen and unheard by humans. Because our own destructive species has so little impact on cave dwellers, they offer a microcosmic study of evolution, a work in progress.

Caves are increasingly being explored by biospeleologists, a new breed of specialists with both caving know-how and scientific training, who venture into the bowels of the earth in pursuit of animals that eke out their existence in utter simplicity. These scientists are armed with research tools that range from infrared thermometers and radio tracking devices for studying bats to nets and jars for capturing aquatic animals and microorganisms. Their assignment: to expose the highly specialized, little-known cave dwellers to unprecedented scientific scrutiny. Their scientific efforts have led to the discovery of many new species and even a genus or two.

Troglobitic cave crabs, Belize

Biospeleologists divide cave denizens into three categories. *Troglophiles* (cave lovers) are versatile creatures able to live out their entire life cycle either on the earth's surface or in caverns. Several species of spiders and crickets are in this category. *Trogloxenes* (cave visitors), such as bats and cave-nesting birds, hang out in caves, taking advantage of the stable environment and the lack of predators, but must leave periodically to forage for food. The hard-core cave dwellers, the ones that never leave, are the *troglobites.*

Though the dark zone of caves would seem to lack creature comforts, many creatures seem to find comfort there. Cave ecologist John R. Holsinger of Old Dominion University in Norfolk, Virginia, estimates more than fifty thousand species of troglobites worldwide, many of them still unknown. He believes that about half of all troglo-

---

Finding residents of the dark zone can be a challenge. Some cave animals spend their lives in nooks and crannies totally inaccessible to humans. But just as bird-watchers have learned to look for different species at various heights in the trees, so students of cave fauna have learned the animals' favorite niches. Spiders, crickets, and bats prefer fairly dry walls and ceilings; flatworms, amphipods, and isopods dwell at the bottom of streams on cave floors; cockroaches, millipedes, and beetles can be found on decomposing flesh of dead cave animals.

In caves that are seldom visited, it's not unusual for a scientist to find the same individual creature in the same small spot year after year. Bats have been recaptured in the same area of the same cave for several years in a row, and one small salamander was seen in the same small crevice almost every week for five straight years. Yet even when a creature's favorite niche is known, gathering samples can be a daunting task. Researchers trying to net Texas blind salamanders have

continued

bites known in North America have been discovered in the past twenty years.

Troglobites, solar rebels, are a varied lot of specialized worms, salamanders, snails, crayfish, isopods, amphipods, spiders, crickets, beetles, and fish. They have evolved from troglophiles that were adapted for subterranean life and then, long ago, became isolated in caves. After millennia of adaptive changes, their progeny became permanent residents. If the species population outside the cave becomes extinct, the cave-dwelling members of that species are said to be in genetic isolation. Ice-age glaciation was probably a major factor in the isolation of the species that became the troglobites found in caves today.

Thanks to natural selection, by which those traits most beneficial to survival are preserved, troglobitic species often display distinctive

descended 50 feet into shafts day after day in search of a single specimen.

Moreover, biospeleologists face the same dangers as other cavers. Once in 1938, in a cave near Springfield, Missouri, Charles Mohr, who would later become president of the National Speleological Society, was so intent on capturing an Ozark blindfish that he failed to notice the rising water in a nearby pool. Retreating to his rope, he was dismayed to discover that the lowest loop, buoyed by the water, was shoulder high and that he couldn't get his foot in it. He called to his partner to get a longer rope. After what seemed like an hour of nervously watching the rising water level, his partner finally dropped a longer rope down, and Mohr began to pull himself up through the torrent of water flowing down the chimney. The force of the cataract jammed his headlamp down over his ears. Upon reaching the halfway point, drenched and exhausted, Mohr began to swing back and forth until he could reach a ledge safe from the full force of the waterfall.

characteristics. Successful creatures in this realm tend to be very efficient in their use of energy. They are smaller and have a slower metabolism and longer life span. They can subsist over long periods on small amounts of food or none at all. Reproduction is timed to coincide with maximum food availability, often an annual flooding of the cave or at least increased stream flow. Troglobites often produce only a few eggs, but these tend to be quite large, providing newborns with a distinct advantage. Similarly, troglobitic species often have a smaller number of larval stages or almost completely bypass the larval stage. This, too, provides a distinct advantage for the species; in a food-poor environment, helpless, immobile larvae would be at a distinct disadvantage in obtaining food and escaping from predators.

Because light detectors would serve no purpose in the dark zone, most troglobites are blind, though some have tiny eyes. They have little or no skin pigmentation (no risk of sunburn) and thin outer coverings. All seem to need far less food than their surface relatives. Still, living in a world of eternal famine, troglobite survival depends above all on their success in finding sustenance, and nearly all of their sensory apparatus and physical resources are devoted to that quest. Any organ unnecessary to this end has degenerated or disappeared entirely. Many have antennae that are longer and more sensitive than those of their surface-dwelling cousins, the better to feel their way around in the dark. They generally have longer legs, allowing them to range farther with less burden on their metabolism. And they tend not to be picky eaters, consuming almost anything that might provide the scantest nourishment.

According to Rick Olsen, ecologist at Mammoth Cave National Park in Kentucky, Mammoth is not only the longest cave system but also the most biologically diverse. More than 130 species call it home, including 15 genuine troglobites, one of which is a shrimp left behind when the ocean receded from Kentucky.

Because no green plants grow in the dark zone, denizens of the deep must get by on food washed in by streams or mud or deposited in bat droppings (guano). Some caves in Mexico and the southwestern United States house colonies of more than a million bats. The guano accumulates on the cave floor, creating a banquet for dozens of species of bottom-feeding troglobites. Guano is a rich food source, and life in guano caves is abundant.

Bones of larger animals thousands of years old have also been found in dark zones. Because of the absence of weathering, entire skeletons of extinct species have sometimes been preserved intact. This is true of the most formidable subterranean beast ever known—*Ursus spelaeus,* the cave bear. Primarily found in Europe, the herbivorous cave bear grew as big as a grizzly. It died out near the end of the last ice age. Since it couldn't possibly have survived on the slim pickings available in the dark zone, it was probably a trogloxene, dependent on the outside environment for food. It no doubt perished because it couldn't adapt to the changes of climate and environment.

Scientists have been able to infer many of the cave bear's habits and characteristics from the vast number of skeletons found in European caves. The clay of one Austrian cavern yielded the remains of thirty thousand bears.

Bats

The most prolific cave denizen, and the most familiar example of the trogloxene, is the bat. It is also the most widely misunderstood. The title of the National Speleological Society brochure on bats is *Bats Need Friends,* and ain't that the truth? Is there a more unfairly maligned mammal on earth? Doubtful.

Widely despised as perpetrators of unspeakable evil, tarnished by legends assassinating their character (the devil is often depicted with bat wings), bats are in fact guilty of nothing more than being ugly and, rarely, causing a case of rabies.

In fact, bats are ecologically indispensable. Most bats in the United States feed on night-flying insects, and they are the only major predator to do so. It has been estimated that a single colony of free-tailed bats in Texas consumes more than 250,000 pounds of insects nightly. That's 125 tons of insects that won't be flitting about your porch light.

There are almost a thousand known species of the order Chiroptera (meaning "hand wing") around the world, thirty-nine of them in the United States, and their diversity is extraordinary. They have exploited all major land habitats on earth except the polar regions, the highest mountains, and some remote islands. They range in size from the smallest bat (and smallest mammal), Kitti's hognosed bat, with a wingspan of 6 inches and weighing as little as .05 ounce, to the largest, the Samoan flying fox, with a reported wingspan of $6^2/_3$ feet and weighing $3^1/_3$ pounds.

Most bats are insectivorous, but some prefer to dine on scorpions, wood lice, shrimp, vertebrates (including mice, lizards, amphibians, fish, and other bats), fruits, flowers, pollen, nectar, or foliage. Some, such as the greater spearnosed bat, are omnivorous, feeding on fruits, insects, and vertebrates. Others specialize; the common vampire bat, for example, subsists its whole life on the blood of mostly one breed of cattle.

Echolocation. The only mammals capable of true flight, bats have developed aerial skills that can rival the most agile birds. Contrary to popular opinion, bats are not blind. Like humans, they have good daylight eyesight but can't see in the dark. To compensate, most species hunt for food at night using echolocation, a complex form of sonar.

For centuries, scientists were baffled by the bat's navigational abilities. The first successful investigation of this mystery was undertaken in 1793 by an Italian, Lazzaro Spallanzani, who discovered that bats could both navigate and feed when blinded. The intrigued Spallanzani wrote that "in the absence of sight there is substituted some new organ or sense, which we do not have and of which consequently we can never have any idea."

Fascinated by the Italian's findings, a Swiss surgeon named Louis Jurine took the research further. He blocked his bats' ears with wax and found that, deprived of their hearing, bats blundered around in the dark as awkwardly as birds.

The mystery persisted, however, because bats made no discernible sound while flying. Some scientists clung to the notion that bats avoided obstacles through a highly developed sense of touch.

In 1920 the recent development of sonar, which located underwater objects by bouncing sound waves off them and measuring distance and direction from the resulting echoes, piqued the interest of British scientist Hamilton Hartridge. Watching a bat dart around his dimly lighted room one night, Hartridge speculated that the agile little animal was guiding itself by the echoes of the sounds it emitted, sounds so high in pitch as to be inaudible to humans.

But Hartridge's arguments remained conjecture until 1938, when two Harvard biology students, Donald Griffin and Robert Galambos, used a sensitive microphone to confirm that bats in flight did indeed produce rapid-fire high-pitched sounds. Subsequent tests proved that when bats neared an obstacle or an edible insect, even one as small as a gnat, the tempo of their squeaks increased.

Using echolocation, bats are prodigious hunters, consuming more than 50 percent of their body weight each night. High-speed photography has caught them on the fly snatching tiny insects in their mouths and larger ones with their wings and tails. The system is not foolproof. Cavers have seen bats collide with newly placed obstacles, leading scientists to conclude that they stop using their sonar once they have memorized a route. After a collision, the advance scouts signal the followers, who then easily avoid the obstacle.

Hibernation. Animals employ different survival strategies when food is scarce or absent. Many bat species hibernate, though not always continuously. Some bats awake every ten days; others may go as long as ninety days.

Physiological changes, such as declines in heartbeat and body temperature, occur during hibernation to help bats eke out energy stores. Although other mammals hibernate, none approach the bat's ability to chill out. The body temperature of most mammal hibernators drops less than 50 degrees Fahrenheit below normal, but the core body temperature of some hibernating bats falls below 32 degrees. Each species has its preferred temperature range. The lowest temperature recorded is 23 degrees F for the red bat. All other things being equal, the lower the body temperature a bat can tolerate, the longer its energy stores will last.

Bats choose their hibernacula, their places of hibernation, based on not only temperature but also humidity. It is critical for all hibernating bats that humidity be high, usually over 90 percent, to minimize evaporation, which would necessitate more frequent awakenings to drink.

Many cave-roosting bats in temperate regions hibernate alone or in small groups. Tropical bats, on the other hand, are more likely to form huge colonies. The little brown and gray bats form clusters of hundreds of thousands of individuals, packed in densities of over 270 per square foot. The purpose of these slumber parties is not understood, as temperatures of individuals within clusters are similar to those of individuals of the same species roosting separately.

Visiting a tropical bat cave can be a disorienting experience, with the masses of bats, the fetid smell of ammonia, and the myriad cockroaches and other species dining on an abundance of guano.

Conservation. Bat populations are declining rapidly worldwide, and several species have recently become extinct, with others endangered. Long considered vermin, countless bats are needlessly destroyed each year. The most serious threats are loss of habitat, human interference, and pesticide poisoning. Cave-dwelling bats are particularly vulnerable to destruction, especially if there is only one small entrance through which all the bats must pass. Hunters and vandals can easily block narrow entrances and trap escaping bats.

A decline in bat populations is destined to have implications far beyond what most people would think. Besides an explosion in insect populations, economic consequences are bound to be great. For example, because of their importance for pollination and seed dispersal, the decline of some flying foxes is having serious effects on crops, tropical forests, and savanna habitats. In Malaysia, colonies of the cave-dwelling dawn bat are threatened with destruction because of limestone quarrying and overexploitation by hunters who rig fishing nets over cave entrances to catch them. Formerly, these bats ranged far and wide to find nectar and pollen, particularly from durian, each hectare of which produced fruit worth $10,000 a year. The decimation of the bat population has been a disaster for durian production.

Fewer bats also mean less guano, which has both ecological and economic consequences. Before Carlsbad Cavern became a national park in 1930, more than one hundred thousand tons of nitrogen-rich guano had been removed by humans and sold as fertilizer. Early cavers described "sinking into a thick, reeking brown substance, not as solid as mud nor as liquid as soup . . . the surface of the vast carpet of guano stirs with life. Wherever you look, insects are feeding on the carcasses of young bats. Thousands of bat skeletons, picked clean to the last shred of flesh, lie all about."

One of the best things you can do to help protect and preserve bats is to leave them alone. This is one of the great problems for cavers, who can inadvertently disturb bat hibernacula. If a bat is disturbed, it will rouse itself, depleting critical fat reserves needed to carry it through hibernation, possibly causing death by starvation. Moreover, bats have strict habitat needs for rearing offspring, and undue disturbance can cause them to permanently abandon a site. Loss of habitat can seriously inhibit species reproduction.

Research and educational efforts by organizations such as the National Speleological Society and Bat Conservation International have played a vital role in raising public awareness of the value of Chiroptera. Bats are now protected by legislation in all European and many other countries. Roost sites and feeding habitats are specially designated. Yet more needs to be done. For more information, or to offer assistance or a tax-deductible donation, contact the following organizations:

Bat Conservation Subcommittee
National Speleological Society
2813 Cave Ave.
Huntsville, AL 35810

Bat Conservation International
Brackenridge Field Laboratory
University of Texas
Austin, TX 78712

The U.S. Government Printing Office in Washington, D.C., publishes a booklet entitled *House Bat Management,* which details ways to cope with bats in homes. According to the booklet, the roosting of bats in a home or garage does not ordinarily constitute a health hazard, unless you pick up a sick bat. Bat phobia has been deliberately generated by the pest-control industry, but in reality the anticoagulant pesticide used to kill bats in houses is a greater health hazard than the bats themselves. If the colony is small, it's usually best to leave the bats undisturbed, letting them earn their keep by catching insects. Unlike mice and rats, they won't chew your possessions or seek human food, and they won't enter an occupied home, except inadvertently. Since most species form only temporary seasonal colonies, you can control guano accumulations in attics by placing plastic sheeting under the roost. Remove it when the bats leave for the season.

If a large colony of bats moves in and you feel you must get rid of them, don't call the exterminator. Many bats roost in inaccessible nooks and crannies, and the corpses of poisoned animals cannot always be removed, creating an unpleasant stench. Also, another colony is liable to move into the vacant roost.

The best solution requires a little effort but is safer and cheaper than hiring an exterminator and will keep a gentle and beneficial resource from being lost. Watch the bats in the evening. When they leave, plug up the access holes so they can't return. Plan your eviction for good weather, so all the bats will be out feeding. Avoid late May to mid-July, when the young are being reared; they are usually left behind in the roost while the adults are out feeding.

It's important to respect and preserve cave life. Many cave species are threatened, and the slightest changes in the cave environment may doom them to extinction. The biggest threats are increased visitation, pollution of cave waters, and decimation of bats by insecticides and other factors. Try not to add to these pressures. Never collect cave life on your own. If you discover something of real interest, notify a local scientist. And sometimes, as a concerned caver, you will just have to turn back. If entering a cave will disturb a hibernating bat colony, do not enter the cave at that time. Mortality is high among bats that are disturbed and forced to fly when food is unavailable. Return later when hibernation is over.

Biology Section of the NSS

The Biology Section of the NSS hosts educational talks and scientific symposia on cave biology. It publishes the *North American Biospeleology Newsletter* several times a year and meets at least once a year at the NSS convention.

Membership is open to all interested persons. Dues are $5 a year. Back issues of the newsletter are available. The current editor is Dr. Daniel Fong, Department of Biology, American University, 4400 Massachusetts Ave., Washington, DC 20016-8007.

The following biospeleologists have agreed to assist or advise serious collectors.

East and Southeast
Dr. John R. Holsinger
Department of Biology
Old Dominion University
Norfolk, VA 23529

Southwest and California
Dr. William R. Elliott
12102 Grimsley Dr.
Austin, TX 78759

West and Pacific
Rod Crawford
University of Washington
Burke Museum (DB-10)
Seattle, WA 98195

Midwest
Dr. Horton H. Hobbs III
Department of Biology
Wittenberg University
Springfield, OH 45501

Hawaii
Dr. Francis G. Howarth
Bishop Museum
P.O. Box 19000A
Honolulu, HI 96817-0916

Mexico and Central America
James R. Reddell
Texas Memorial Museum
2400 Trinity St.
Austin, TX 78705

METEOROLOGY

Temperature

In contrast to outside temperatures, many caves feel pleasantly cool in the summer and warm in the winter. This can be deceptive, for temperate cave temperatures usually range from cool to cold. Add a little air movement and a little water, and the result is a chill factor that intensifies the cold for the caver.

Within the depths of a single cave, the air temperature remains pretty constant throughout the year. Most inner caves fluctuate 2 degrees F or less. Air temperature is greatly determined by wall temperature, which is approximately equal to the mean annual temperature outside the cave. Daily and seasonal temperature fluctuations aboveground are damped underground by layers of rock and soil. An aboveground temperature fluctuation of 30 degrees F is reduced to 1 degree F at a depth of about 40 feet.

As mean surface temperatures vary greatly from place to place, so do cave temperatures. Both latitude and altitude are important factors in predicting cave temperatures. In general, the higher the latitude or elevation, the colder the cave. Caves near the Canadian border average about 41 degrees F and those near the Mexican border about 68 degrees F. For every 1,000 feet of vertical climb, figure to lose almost 4 degrees F. Thus, caves located at high altitudes or latitudes, where the mean temperature is below freezing, may contain permanent ice.

Cave temperatures can also be influenced by water movement. Consider a single-entrance cave with a stream flowing forcefully through the entrance and on into the cave passage. The friction created by water flowing through air drags air along above the surface of the water, a process called *entrainment.* The result is low-level air movement into the cave passage. But if air is moving in, it also must be moving out at higher levels. In cases of rapid flooding, the incoming water displaces air, causing strong, outward-flowing air. The greater the amount of air exchange between a cave and the outside, the greater the variations in temperature and humidity within the cave. Several factors affect air movement.

Air moves into and out of caves as a way of maintaining a pressure balance between the cave air and the external air. During the day, outside air is usually warmed, which means it's less dense and therefore has lower barometric pressure. At night the outside air is cooled and barometric pressure rises. In this way, there are continual adjustments taking place between the cave air near the entrance and the outside air. This drive toward a balance in pressure, or homeostasis, results in air movement into the cave at night and out during the day. Major weather changes can also affect barometric pressure, which will influence air flow near cave entrances.

Sometimes lack of air flow is the dominant meteorological condition. In single-entrance caves where winters are cold, cold air may sink to the cave's lowest levels and, if water is present, cause ice to form. The summer's warm air may be incapable of displacing the heavier cold air in the cave, resulting in permanent ice, even though the area's annual mean temperature is above freezing.

Caves with multiple entrances at different levels may exhibit what is called the *chimney effect* in response to temperature differentials between inside and outside air. Such temperature variations create an air pressure difference at the lower cave opening, and air flows either into or out of the cave to restore the balance. Cold air will flow out of the cave's lower entrance when the cave air is colder than the air outside the entrance. As cold air flows out of the lower entrance, warmer air flows into the upper entrance. Conversely, when the cave air is warmer than the outside air, cooler air will flow into the lower entrance as comparatively warm cave air flows out of the upper entrance.

Thus, caves displaying the chimney effect are subject to seasonal changes in air flow. Typically, air flows out of the lower entrance in the summer and into the lower entrance in the winter. In spring and fall, when cave and external temperatures are nearly the same, there may be daily changes in air direction caused by changes in diurnal and nocturnal outside air temperatures. Caves subject to the chimney effect that display persistent winds are often called *blowing caves*.

Humidity

In most limestone caves, water seeps through walls, ceilings, and floors, saturating the cave air with water vapor. Relative humidity, the ratio of water vapor actually in the air at a certain temperature to the amount of water vapor needed to saturate the air at that temperature, approaches 100 percent in the depths of damp caves. This is not the case near cave entrances, however, where unsaturated air may be entering the cave from outside.

The temperature of the entering air will gradually change as it is cooled or warmed by contact with the cave walls. Cold air cannot hold as much water vapor as warm air. Thus, if air entering a cave is cooled, its relative humidity rises; if it is warmed, its relative humidity falls. In summer, then, warm air entering a cave soon reaches 100 percent relative humidity, as the cooler cave walls lower its temperature. In winter, incoming air with a temperature lower than the cave walls will be slowly warmed by the rock and may not attain 100 percent relative humidity for a long time. Depending upon whether the cave walls are cooler or warmer than the dew point of the air, moisture will be either evaporated from or condensed on the walls where this temperature differential exists.

Even talented, experienced cave explorers never lose their respect for Mother Nature. Low temperatures, wind, and cold water can be killers, but not for the prepared, cautious, and intelligent caver.

ARCHAEOLOGY

Archaeology is the scientific study of the remains of past human societies, both the physical or biological aspects and the social or cultural aspects. Although archaeologists do work in caves, very few are familiar with the deep-cave environment. Most true cave finds have been in the twilight zone, although exceptions abound. Early humans created art in the dark zone of Altamira Cave in Spain. These cave dwellers may also have worshiped in them. Dozens of caves containing paintings, pictographs, and statues up to twenty thousand years old have been found in the Dordogne Valley of France, site of the famous Grotte de Lascaux.

The world's longest cave, Mammoth in Kentucky, was extensively explored prehistorically and has yielded a bounty of archaeological remains. Between 1000 B.C. and 500 A.D., Native Americans mined Mammoth and other caves in the eastern United States for a variety of minerals. Over the years, they left behind large quantities of artifacts that were preserved in the stable environment, such as gourd and squash bowls, woven bags and slippers, and even a few mummies.

Our semierect and erect ancestors have been leaving their mark on the planet for millions of years, yet written history has recorded only parts of the last five thousand years. Archaeologists are forever trying to fill that immense gap with knowledge, and we all lose whenever a site is destroyed before it can be studied. Chances are, if you cave long enough, you will see, if not discover, archaeological remains that suggest explorers were there hundreds or even thousands of years before. The evidence may be subtle, so you must be observant. Be especially vigilant in dry upper-level passages or in hydrologically abandoned caves. You might find a footprint preserved in dried mud, charcoal remnants, smudges on the walls or ceiling, or faint drawings etched in the mud or limestone. Some of these clues will be off the beaten track, or they may be hidden by breakdown, covered with trash, or trampled by years of traffic.

If you discover a virgin or little-traveled passage, tread carefully, especially if the cave is known to harbor prehistoric remains in other passages. Footprints or drawings etched in mud are extremely delicate. A single careless caver can easily obliterate a rich record of past life that has existed for thousands of years. Be a conscientious caver and help preserve such remains for future study and for other cavers to see.

2

History of Caving

For most of human history, the deep zone of caves has been associated with magic and mystery. Cavemen—Cro-Magnon and his predecessors—established their living quarters near the entrances but seldom ventured far inside. Later, mythology often placed gods, saints, and heroes in caves: Zeus was born in a cave, and the Japanese sun goddess Amaterasu hid in a cave, plunging the world into darkness. Mythological caves also were inhabited by trolls, gnomes, and hobgoblins.

Even the ancient sages, striving to replace superstition with rational thought, couldn't always overcome their cave phobias. The poet Virgil said of caves, "There is something supernatural here." The Roman philosopher Seneca described a cave visited by a party of Greek silver prospectors in words that will never be quoted on cave brochures: "They saw huge rushing rivers and vast still lakes, spectacles fit to make them shake with horror. The land hung above their heads and the winds whistled hollowly in the shadows. In the depths, the frightful rivers led nowhere into the perpetual and alien night." After the miners returned to the surface, he added, "they live in fear, for tempting the fires of Hell."

A seventeenth-century English writer worried that his planned visit to a Somerset cavern would permanently alter his personality. "Although we entered in frolicksome and merry, yet we might return out of it Sad and Pensive, and never more be seen to Laugh whilst we lived in the world." In a 1689 engraving, the Austrian explorer and artist Baron Johann Valvasor depicted the stalagmite and dripstone formations inside Adelsberg Cave as hideous gargoyles and monsters.

The fear and revulsion that caves inspired in otherwise rational people were especially understandable before the widespread availability of carbide and electric lamps in the first part of the twentieth century. Strange apparitions always seemed to loom just beyond the reach of the glow cast by torch or candle. Add to that the unfamiliar sound of water spilling through rocky corridors, the slippery ooze of mud in crawlways, and the deep pits lying in wait for the unwary, and the subterranean world offered up more than enough intimidating obstacles to dissuade the masses. The early few who did venture underground had purposes other than adventure. For example, fortune hunters explored German caves in the sixteenth and seventeenth centuries in search of unicorn horns, which purportedly had great medicinal value.

The first cavern to achieve worldwide fame as a showplace was Adelsberg Cave, located near the Austrian village of the same name. Explorers began probing it as early as the thirteenth century, but notoriety was assured in 1818 when Holy Roman Emperor Francis I decided to see its reputed wonders firsthand.

In anticipation of the royal visit, workers cleared away rubble and installed torches. In a far wall, 90 feet above the floor, a worker discovered a gap. Crawling through the opening, he found a whole new section, dominated by an amphitheater much larger than the first, with galleries of fantastic dripstone formations.

The emperor declined the crawlspace, but local officials decided to make this new area accessible to the public. Workers leveled paths through the chambers, built a wooden bridge across the cave's underground river, and chiseled stone stairs into the walls. Chandeliers and lanterns replaced the torches, and guides were trained. By the 1870s Adelsberg was drawing eight thousand tourists a year, and a fashionable hotel had been built nearby to house and feed the wealthiest of them.

In America, caves were valued more for their economic than their aesthetic worth. For thousands of years, Native Americans in the Kentucky karst belt, the most extensive cave region on the continent, had mined gypsum, which they used in ceremonial paints. By the late eighteenth century, settlers on the rugged western frontier were extracting saltpeter from caves. A vital ingredient in gunpowder, saltpeter was found in nitrate-laden cave soil enriched by the guano of generations of bats.

In the 1790s, the legend goes, a hunter named John Houchin tracked a wounded bear to its lair in the wooded hills of central Kentucky. After killing the bear, Houchin entered its cave and found a huge chamber, its walls black with bats. The cave floor was thick with nitrate-rich bat guano, which radiated an acrid ammonia stench. The War of 1812 boosted the demand for saltpeter. The cave property changed hands several times, its value appreciating with each sale. One owner, who boasted that the cave "could supply the whole globe with saltpeter," changed its name to Mammoth Cave. It was destined to become as famous in America as Adelsberg was in Europe.

FLOYD COLLINS

Only once in history has a cave story been front-page news all over the world. This is that story.

In the 1920s, the so-called Cave Wars of central Kentucky were fueled by a bitter rivalry between venerable Mammoth Cave, the biggest in the world, and nearby smaller caves whose owners objected to Mammoth's domination of the tourist market. Rival billboards touted "Kentucky's Most Beautiful Cave" and "The Greatest Cave of All." Vociferous hucksters for the various attractions roamed the streets handing out flyers, sometimes leaping onto running boards to deliver their spiels. Spies were planted, fights broke out, property was destroyed.

One small but exquisite competitor was Great Crystal Cave, discovered by a local lad named Floyd Collins. Collins was a lean, hollow-cheeked, uneducated cave-country native. A man of few words and few friends, he often seemed more at home underground than on top of it.

After years of discovering and exploring caves that were either too small or too ordinary to be commercially profitable, he had found the cavern of his dreams in 1917, when he was thirty. Two weeks of hard digging had uncovered a passage leading to a 65-foot-high room festooned with hundreds of white and cream-colored gypsum flowers. Several other magnificent chambers lay beyond it.

Unfortunately, Great Crystal failed to prosper. It was at the end of an unimproved road, far from the main highway, past several other caves. So Collins made a deal with Beesley Doyle, the owner of some strategically placed land. Collins would do the back-breaking labor necessary to find a worthy cave, and they would split any profits. Collins had already spotted a sinkhole on the property, and it was there that he began digging. He was partly motivated by dreams of commercial success, but the driving force in Collins's life was a love—some would say a mania—for exploring beautiful caves. Floyd Collins approached caving with the fervor of a religious fanatic.

He spent three laborious weeks clearing rocky debris from the narrow, twisting, downward-sloping shaft. By Friday, January 30, 1925, he sensed a major breakthrough was imminent. The day before, he had set some dynamite and cleared the ensuing rubble, and this day he was sure that he would find a world-class cavern.

It was a drizzly morning. Water dripped everywhere, and the winter runoff was in full flush. Except for the old kerosene lantern he carried and the 72-foot rope slung over his shoulder, Collins could have been a farmer out inspecting crop damage.

He reached the cave entrance and looked around. There was no one in sight. There never was. He dropped to all fours and slithered into what would become known as Sand Cave. The entrance passage sloped slightly downward for about 15 feet, followed by a 4-foot drop to a small hole. Floyd deftly lowered his slender frame through the hole, then dropped to his hands and knees as the passageway doubled back under itself. The tube then twisted and turned between a jumble of limestone blocks, before it narrowed to a squeeze that forced Floyd to wriggle against the ceiling and walls in order to inch his 160-pound body through. A slightly larger person would not have made it.

Angled downward about 10 degrees, the tube shrank to 10 inches high, bending sharply to the right, before it reached an alcove barely big enough for Collins to turn around. A few feet farther lay a narrow pitlike chute that dropped 10 feet to a shallow cubbyhole and then a diagonal body-sized crevice. Thanks to the previous day's dynamite, Collins could finally get beyond the bottom of the chute and into the crevice.

Pushing the kerosene lamp and rope ahead of him, he wriggled through the diagonal crevice, noting that the walls and ceiling were not solid bedrock but consisted of loose dirt and protruding rocks. One ominous-looking stone jutted from the ceiling at the narrowest part of the tunnel. Estimating that it weighed about 100 pounds, Collins deftly eased past it.

He emerged onto a ledge overlooking a 60-foot pit. Fixing his rope, he rappelled down and investigated the bottom of the hole. Suddenly his lantern flickered, warning him to turn back. After ascending the rope, he left it fixed for his anticipated return. Then he crawled headfirst into the body-sized crevice, earthworming his way forward with his hips, shoulders, and stomach, and digging his feet into the floor and walls to push off. The earth surrounded him like a cocoon, but such confinement didn't bother him as it did most people.

Collins was now 115 feet from the cave's entrance and 55 feet beneath the surface. Before trying to ascend from the crevice into the cubbyhole, he shoved his lantern up ahead. Suddenly it fell over and went out, cloaking him in darkness. It was annoying, but no more than that; he had been in cave blackouts before, and besides, he knew the way home.

With his arms pinned to his sides and his feet braced against the floor and walls of the tube, he pushed off to gain momentum. As sightless as a troglobite, he accidentally struck the large rock that protruded from the ceiling. It dislodged and fell on his left ankle, pinning it. He kicked out with his right leg but only managed to break down more dirt and stones, which now immobilized his right foot. His hands still at his sides, he worked his stomach and thigh muscles, trying to squirm free. But every move just brought down more debris, further entombing Collins in dirt and rock.

Finally he lay still, panting and sweating profusely. He was lying on his left side at a 45-degree angle, his head in the cubbyhole at the bottom of a 10-foot chute. His arms were straitjacketed at his sides and his legs were encased in cave detritus. A trickle of water dripped from a limestone boulder onto his cheek. It was cave-dark. Collins was confronting one of mankind's most deeply rooted fears—being buried alive.

Panic welled up in his throat. Shivering in the damp 54-degree chill, he began to cry for help. He knew the chances were nil that anyone would hear him, but he had to do something. He screamed until his voice went out, then fell into a fitful doze, comforted by only one thought: At least his partner, Beesley Doyle, knew where he was.

It wasn't until the next morning that Doyle and two other men arrived at the cave entrance. Only seventeen-year-old Jewell Estes was slim enough to attempt the passage. As the young man squirmed deeper and deeper underground, he tremulously called Floyd's name. At last he heard a muffled reply: "Come to me. I'm hung up." Muddy, chilled, and afraid, Jewell retreated for help.

When the news of Floyd's plight reached the Collins farmhouse, his brothers Marshall and Homer rushed to the scene. Marshall was unable to reach Floyd, but twenty-two-year-old Homer, the youngest of the five brothers and, next to Floyd, the most experienced caver, stripped to his underwear and managed to get by both squeezes and down the narrow chute to where Floyd had lain without food, water, and light for more than twenty-four hours.

"Floyd, you all right?" called Homer.

"That's my old buddy Homer," Floyd cried. "I knowed you'd be comin' down to help me!"

But Homer soon confronted the problem that would frustrate every would-be rescuer: Enter the chute headfirst and you were forced to work upside down, able to exit only by pushing feetfirst up the steep slope. Enter feetfirst, as Homer had done, and you couldn't reach Floyd to dig without contorting yourself into Houdinilike positions.

Homer was appalled by Floyd's plight, but he kept a brave face. He stuffed burlap bags around his brother's body and over his face to shield him from the dripping water. Floyd said he was hungry, so Homer called up for food and then began the agonizingly slow process of digging out the dirt and rocks that covered Floyd to the shoulders. When the food came, Homer had to feed his brother like a baby, which only made the situation seem more dire. After Floyd had consumed nine sausage sandwiches and a pint of coffee, Homer returned to digging, laboriously filling a syrup can and passing it up to a chain of helpers for disposal. Toiling through the night, he succeeded in uncovering his brother's torso and upper arms.

Finally, cold, weary, and despondent over the slow progress, Homer had to return to the surface to rest and warm himself by one of the fires that burned there. While Homer fortified himself, others entered the cave intending to offer help. But all were thwarted by the mud, the clammy chill, the pinched crawlways, and the oppressive terror that the cave inspired. Not one of them reached Floyd, though one local farmer did get close enough to talk to him. "I'm trapped, and trapped for life," Floyd told him.

At the top of the chute, the crowd swelled to a hundred. When Floyd's father, old man Lee, began a rambling monologue suggesting that Floyd's entrapment was God's will, it provoked a bitter argument with Homer and Marshall. Amid the chaos, Marshall offered $500 to anyone who would go in the cave and rescue his brother. The crowd buzzed with excitement, but there were no takers.

Returning to the cave around 5:00 Sunday afternoon, Homer scooped out more dirt until he uncovered Floyd's hands, which were still pinned at his sides. He managed to slip a crowbar into Floyd's left hand and urged him to try to pry loose the rock that lay on his ankle, but Floyd was too weak to move it. Meanwhile, Homer dug, trying to chisel away the hard ceiling limestone to give himself more room, but his progress could be measured in millimeters. It was like trying to mine ore with a butter knife.

By midnight Sunday, two and a half days after Floyd's entrapment, all rescue efforts had stalled. It was a grim tableau at the top, with more than a hundred people huddled in the rain around sputtering campfires, discussing rescue prospects, tippling moonshine, and trying to ward off the dampness. Water now stood 2 or 3 inches deep in some sections of the passage, making descent into the cave even more miserable.

Thus far, only Homer had been active in the cave. Convinced that he could rely on no one else, he returned to his brother around

2:30 A.M. Floyd was cold, shaky, and drifting in and out of reality. Homer stayed with him through the night, listening as his tortured brother ranted on about everything from angels to chicken sandwiches. "Oh God, Homer," he groaned at one point, "please take me home to bed."

By Monday, February 2, newspapers across the country had picked up the Collins story, and journalists at the scene were now mingling with cave-country locals. One writer who would play a leading role in the drama was the Louisville *Courier-Journal*'s William B. "Skeets" Miller. A jockey-sized 5-foot-5 and 117 pounds, Miller looked younger than his twenty-one years. Approaching Homer, who was warming himself by a fire after his third descent into Sand Cave, Miller asked him for information. "If you want information," Homer snapped, fed up with outsiders in general and reporters in particular, "there's the hole right over there. You can go down and find out for yourself." Surprising even himself, Miller accepted the challenge. "I guess," he said later, "I was ashamed not to." It was a decision that would change the course of his life.

Miller put on a pair of overalls and started down. He was immediately struck by how cramped, still, dark, and damp it was. A spooky kind of loneliness permeated the cave, and terror threatened to immobilize him at every turn. As much to settle his nerves as to elicit a response, he called Floyd's name every few seconds.

After slithering through the turnaround, Miller entered the chute. Suddenly out of control, he slid headfirst for several feet, losing his flashlight and colliding with a wet lump that groaned and moved. Nearly paralyzed with fear, Miller tried to scramble away from the lump, but the steep incline held him back. Just then he heard another groan and realized the lump was Collins.

Shaken to his core, Miller found his flashlight and scrambled back up to the turnaround. After spending a moment calming his nerves, he reentered feetfirst. As he got closer, Collins asked Miller to turn off his flashlight because it hurt his eyes.

Miller took stock of the poor man's position. He was appalled; it was hard to imagine a more terrifying plight. Nearly overcome with nausea, he fought a recurring desire to flee. He lifted the piece of burlap that Homer had placed over his brother's face to keep the dripping water from torturing him. "Put it back," Floyd said weakly. "The water."

On that first trip, Miller spent only ten minutes with Collins. "As I saw it," he later wrote, "nothing would accomplish his release. Reaching him with food would only prolong his agony. Each hour he remained made him less able to help himself. His position was such that those who could reach him only filled the passage above him and could not do much toward rescuing him."

Following an arduous uphill scramble, Skeets Miller stumbled out into the light. He was exhausted, shivering, and covered in mud from head to toe. Emotions flooded his soul. His exhilarating relief at being free of the cave was matched by his pity for Collins. He sank down with his head between his knees and cried.

By Tuesday, February 3, the Collins story was front-page news in almost every newspaper in the country. The *New York Times* carried Collins's entrapment as one of its lead stories. Each morning, Americans were greeted with huge, often exaggerated, headlines: "CAVE VICTIM NEAR RELEASE," "KENTUCKIAN TRAPPED ALIVE BY 7-TON BOULDER," "MAN UNDER GROUND 80 HOURS STILL LIVES."

At the cave entrance, reporters and photographers jostled for position with locals and a growing mass of curious onlookers. The dreadful anguish of a man who could be touched, fed, comforted, but not freed tapped some emotional wellspring, a combination of dread and empathy. Like other human tragedies, it brought out both the best and the worst in people. One gas station attendant in nearby Cave City caught the irony of Floyd's plight with this remark: "People are funny. Fellas that wouldn't have lent Floyd fifty cents are pert near killin' themselves goin' down that hole to pull him out."

Despite Skeets Miller's feelings of repulsion and futility, he refused to quit. Compassion and a sense of duty drove him back into the cave Tuesday afternoon. This time he crawled through the black ooze dragging a long cord with light bulbs pigtailed to it. The extra light dispelled some of the terror of the cave. It also allowed him to use both hands to try to dig out Collins. Operating in a space about the size of a dining room chair, he twisted his body into near-impossible positions, eventually clawing away enough dirt and gravel to expose Floyd's left knee. He labored in agony; sharp rocks tore at his hands and punctured his body, and Miller was soon drenched in sweat. Finally he could do no more and sat panting in the bottom of the pit. The volunteers strung out in the cave above him, by now numbed by the wet and cold, sent down coffee, milk, and whiskey, then retreated to the surface.

Arranging himself so that Floyd's head rested on his knee, Miller fed the prisoner through a soda straw that he pinched shut when Collins had to swallow. The light was a comfort to both men, infusing them with a sense of comradeship, and Floyd was uncharacteristically lucid and talkative.

Thus began the most remarkable interview in the history of American journalism. Never before had a reporter been able to touch and talk to someone who was so hopelessly buried alive. "I was mighty weak a few hours ago, mighty weak," Collins said, "but now I feel better."

Then Collins began to describe what it was like to be trapped alive, including the emotional roller coaster that accompanied each rescue attempt. Oh, how relieved he'd been when first discovered. And how disappointed when his brothers failed to free him. "I prayed as hard's I could. I begged God to send help to me," he said.

Monday had been a day of hope. For the first time, strangers visited him, giving him the feeling that something was being accomplished. When he was alone, he had spurts of intense effort when he would marshal his strength, hunch his shoulders, tighten his stomach muscles, and claw at the ground trying to free himself. At times his thoughts slipped back to the possibility of the limestone rock above him giving way and crushing him. "I kept tryin' to drive my mind to somethin' else, but it wa'nt much use," he said.

Monday night had been hell. His foot had pained terribly, as though it were going to break off. He sometimes cried inconsolably. As one rescue attempt after another failed, he began to pray constantly.

He told Miller that his first thoughts on Tuesday morning were "Four days down here and no nearer freedom than I was the first day. How will it end?" "I've faced death afore," he confided to Miller. "It don't frighten me none. But it's so long . . . so long."

Skeets read Floyd several telegrams from well-wishers, assuring him that prayers were being said for him all over the country. "It's mighty fine to know so many people are pullin' for me," Floyd smiled weakly. "Tell 'em I love 'em all."

Up on top, rescue attempts were bogged down in acrimony. A huge crowd had formed, but it lacked leadership, a chain of command. One man offered to torch the rock around Collins, but the consensus was that it would burn the victim. Others favored sinking a separate shaft, but that was rejected as too time-consuming. Amputation was considered and a surgeon called in, but that was eventually rejected as inhumane. Meanwhile, Floyd Collins was in a living hell.

Johnnie Gerald, Floyd's friend and caving companion, had his own opinions about the proper direction of the rescue effort. "Stabilize the existing passageway, keep Floyd warm, dry, and fed, and dig him out," he argued. In the next couple of days, Gerald would make several subterrancan trips to see Floyd, but the digging was unbearably slow.

A Louisville Fire Department lieutenant briefly held sway with his plan to strap a harness to Collins and yank him free by rope. Skeets Miller was able to strap on the harness, but as the rope tightened, Floyd began to scream, "Don't do it! Stop! I can't stand it! It's pulling me in two! Stop them! Oh God, stop them!" And finally they did.

Next they tried to pry up the rock with an automobile jack and a crowbar. Again, Skeets Miller was the point man in an underground human chain. Descending the shaft yet again, he wedged a crowbar next to the rock and braced a screw jack against the sloping ceiling, but the jack was too big for the confined space. Another jack was passed down, but it was too small. Miller called down for wooden blocks to fill the space between the crowbar handle and the jack. Once they were in place, he began slowly turning the screw. The crowbar moved, the rock moved. "Keep turning, fella. It's coming off!" Floyd yelled euphorically. Miller too felt a surge of exhilaration, but two more turns caused the blocks to slip out. Miller tried again, but again the blocks slipped. "Try it again, try it again," Floyd pleaded. Miller once more piled the blocks in position and began jacking, but once more they slid out of position.

Sweating and chilled to the bone, Miller was spent. Floyd suggested he go get some rest and try again later. Miller arranged a burlap-wrapped light bulb on Floyd's chest and left, sick at heart. As word of this last failure was passed up the passageway, several of the men in the tunnel felt like crying. Miller would later berate himself for not trying to affix the blocks with wire or tape.

Shortly after the weary Miller resurfaced, two miners crawled down the passageway and returned with the ominous news that cracks were developing in the ceiling at the top of the chute. Other men sent in to investigate came back with even worse news: The ceiling had caved in about 15 feet above Collins; it was now impossible to reach him.

Johnnie Gerald went back in Wednesday evening (day six) to see the breakdown for himself. He was fuming, having warned that the amateurish activities of outsiders were bound to cause cave damage. When Gerald reached the breakdown, he discussed with another man the possibility of digging out the rubble. Down below, Floyd heard Gerald's voice but not his words.

"Johnnie, Johnnie, is that you? Come to me! Why don't someone come to me?"

Gerald stalled. "Some rocks have fallen, and we will, Floyd, we will. First, we got to dig 'em out."

"Johnnie . . . Oh, God . . . help me . . ." Floyd fell into an uncontrolled sobbing. "Oh Lord, dear Lord, Jesus all powerful . . . save me . . . Johnnie . . . Johnnie . . ." Unable to stand it any longer, Gerald had to leave.

He returned once more to dig out rubble, but a 40-pound rock fell from the ceiling and struck his spine, ending his rescue efforts. "I'm done," he said to a companion. "My nerve's gone."

Another man led an attempt to claw through the breakdown, but progress was negligible. "Don't give up," he shouted to Floyd, "we're coming."

"You're too slow," came the dispirited monotone from below. "Too slow."

By the seventh day of Floyd's entrapment, he was in worse shape than ever. No longer could he be supplied with food and water (although, as some would note, he could've been provided with a feeding tube before the breakdown). The *Nashville Tennessean,* with a devoted readership, ran gossip as news. They exhibited an eight-column headline: "Dog to Be Sent with Food to Collins in Cave." The paper neglected to explain how Floyd was supposed to get the provisions off the dog, assuming the animal could even reach him. On February 7, the *Atlanta Constitution* stretched the truth even further, reporting that the dog crept into the tunnel a few feet, "found an old bone which he began to chew on, and refused to go further."

Having reached a dead end in the main passageway, the rescuers began to focus their efforts on excavating a vertical shaft. Engineers estimated that the shaft would have to pierce 55 feet of dirt and limestone to reach Collins. Because of the high risk of cave-ins, diggers would have to rely on picks and shovels rather than explosives, and no one would be allowed in the cave.

One week after Collins's entrapment, teams of volunteers, many of them miners, began to dig a 6-foot-square shaft about 20 feet from the cave entrance. Estimates of how long it would take to reach Collins ranged from the optimistic (two or three days) to the incredible (a few hours).

By Friday, they were 10 feet down, but the pace soon slowed as the sides of the shaft began to spill dirt into the pit. As volunteer diggers inched downward, the mass of onlookers swelled to festival proportions. By Sunday, the throng that massed at Sand Cave was estimated at ten thousand. Floyd's sixty-five-year-old father, Lee, moved through the crowd passing out leaflets touting the wonders of the family's Great Crystal Cave. Tents pitched in the muddy clearing housed a field hospital, a kitchen for the workmen, and other support facilities. "It looked like a country fair," the *New York Times* observed. "Hot-dog vendors, dealers in apples and soda pop, sandwich makers and jugglers vied for the nickels and dimes of the thousands."

The diggers, working in continuous shifts, reached 50 feet on Friday the thirteenth. Two of them reported hearing a cough, and it was soon heard all around the world. The tension was becoming unbearable. Newspapers had been predicting an imminent breakthrough for days. By Saturday, the fourteenth, two weeks and one day after Floyd Collins's entrapment, the shaft was 55 feet deep, and the men started digging a lateral tunnel in the direction they expected him to be. By noon Monday, the tunnel extended just over 12 feet.

The shout from the end of the tunnel was electrifying: "We're there!" Finally, an opening was scratched out wide enough to allow volunteer Ed Brenner to squeeze through. While others held his feet, Brenner beamed his flashlight into the dark until he saw a man's head 6 feet below. He stared for a few seconds, until he realized that Floyd's face was a frozen mask of despair. After Brenner was pulled out, he uttered but a single word: "Dead."

The nation mourned a man known to only a few people before he became a victim. Because the diggers had intersected the shaft above him, they still could not extricate the body. While Floyd still lay where he was entrapped, a minister 60 feet above conducted a funeral service, eulogizing Collins as a lover of caves "who saw in the gigantic formations and in the fantastic patterns on the wall the traceries of God."

Two months later, a party of miners hired by Homer Collins dug farther down the rescue shaft and removed Floyd's body. They also extracted the rock that had first trapped him. Described in various fictionalized news accounts as weighing up to 7 tons, it actually tipped the scale at 27 pounds.

THE AGE OF EXPLORATION

The achievements of early explorers were limited not by their daring but by their equipment. Before the middle of the twentieth century, cavers making a vertical descent would anchor a hemp rope at the surface and climb down hand over hand, trusting their lives to their own strong arms and shoulders. The long rope climb back up was even more taxing.

Technology greatly increased the range of cavers. Instead of lighting their way with a flickering candle or lantern, they adopted the helmet-mounted carbide and electric lamps favored by miners. Hemp ropes, easily frayed by sharp cave rocks and subject to rotting in the damp underground environment, were replaced by strong nylon lines, and flimsy rope ladders gave way to flexible aluminum rungs suspended on steel cables. In Europe, mechanical winches were sometimes used for long vertical drops.

Cavers began to borrow techniques and hardware from mountaineers and rock climbers. The first such adaptation, for vertical rope ascents, was a knot designed for avalanche rescue by Austrian mountaineer Karl Prusik around 1930. The prusik knot slid easily up a rope but tightened sufficiently under downward pressure to hold a climber's weight. By attaching foot loops to a vertical rope with a prusik knot, a climber or caver could walk slowly up the rope, sliding the knotted foot loops upward one at a time. Later, in caving, as in mountain climbing, mechanical ascenders replaced the prusik knot, and a device called a rappel rack was invented for controlled one-rope descents.

With improved equipment came advances in technique and style. Serious cave explorers began to realize the need to use teamwork to push subterranean frontiers. In order to pool their knowledge, European and American cavers organized themselves into clubs and federations. In 1941 the National Speleological Society was chartered in the United States, and soon caving societies began to bloom throughout the western world. Within a decade, well-organized expeditions had replaced the solitary ramblings of previous generations.

These expeditions were systematic and purposeful. Using compasses to determine direction of movement, clinometers to measure angles of descent and ascent, and altimeters to calculate depth, teams of scientist-explorers meticulously charted every passage they found. They returned year after year to the same caves to probe promising leads.

This technical revolution contributed mightily to the fledgling science of caves. Called speleology, it encompasses the study of cave geology, geography, biology, and history. It may also include the study of karst (limestone) topography and groundwater hydrology, the flow of water through caves.

There have been impressive speleological gains since World War II, leading to unifying principles regarding the origin, age, and history of caves, the cave environment, the prehistoric peoples who inhabited them, and the life cycles of cave animals. Through the synergism of science and exploration, cavers continue to go deeper and farther. Humans have clawed their way more than a mile deep. Explored passages in the Mammoth Cave system increase by about a mile a month and, as of this writing, stand at about 350 miles.

One of the exciting things about cave exploration is that the limits are unknown. We know Everest is the highest mountain on earth, but is Mammoth really the longest cave or reseau Jean Bernard the deepest? Unlike glaciers, mountains, oceans, or other surface features, caves are secret places undetectable by satellite scans or airborne instruments. The earth's underground cavities offer what is truly the last frontier for serious explorers.

Despite huge advances in equipment, technique, and accomplishments, little has happened in caving to alter the essential message of noted Swiss speleologist Alfred Bogli, who in 1966 wrote: "Under the earth's crust there exists such an enormously great world, in absolute darkness, that we can with some justice speak of a new continent."

3

Personal Cave Gear and Clothing

To explore your first horizontal or semihorizontal cave, all you really need is a hard hat, lighting, a good pair of boots, and some old clothes.

CLOTHING

Although there is no official uniform, your choice of outfits is critical. It must protect your body from rocks and jagged edges, be loose enough to permit a wide range of movements, and maintain an equilibrium between heat gain and loss. In general, cave clothes should keep you warm during prolonged periods of inactivity but not be so bulky that they restrict movement during crawling or climbing. They should also be free of loops, belts, or floppy pockets that can catch on projections.

The same basic rules of layering apply to cavers as to climbers and backpackers. Because air is trapped and kept warm between each layer, two thin sweaters are more effective than one thick one. With several layers of warm clothing available, you can add or subtract to achieve the warmth needed. This provides maximum flexibility during temperature fluctuations. Taking off clothes during a warm spell is a minor inconvenience, but not having enough clothing when you're wet or cold can be a major disaster.

Inner Layer

The inner layer should offer insulation and wick moisture from the body. Cotton, a moisture absorber, is great in hot weather but not so great in cool caves. Wool retains its warmth when wet but can be unbearably scratchy. The greatest advance in textiles for outdoor adventurers in the past decade has been the development of light-weight, high-performance polyester underwear. Miracle fabrics like polypropylene, Thermax, and Capilene are perfect for the inner sock and underwear layer. They wick away moisture and are stretchy enough to permit radical movements. They are machine washable, and the moisture-moving quality won't wash out.

Outer Layer

The outer layer for climbers and backpackers is often a rainproof shell, but cavers, who are protected from rain and are hard on their clothes, usually prefer coveralls. As the name suggests, coveralls cover your pants and shirt and keep them in place. This is more important than you might suppose when crawling through tight places. Sometimes in warm caves coveralls are omitted, but this may be a mistake, as they also help keep pockets and loose clothing from snagging on rocks.

Cavers in coveralls

Boots

Choose coveralls with buttons or Velcro, as cave mud has been known to penetrate and paralyze zippers. Look for coveralls in heavy material with reinforced knees and seat. The seat is often the first part to wear out. Consider adding butt and knee patches of your own; cut pieces of 1/8-inch Ensolite to fit into pockets sewed into the coveralls. This allows easy removal of the pads during washing.

Boots

Wearing improper or worn-out shoes places added stress on your hips, knees, ankles, and feet, where up to 90 percent of all sports injuries occur. Choose shoes suitable for your activity and replace them before they wear out and lose their shock-absorbing ability.

People have entered caves wearing a lot of different types of footwear, many of them inappropriate. Athletic shoes—tennis, running, and cross-training—should be avoided in favor of some type of boot.

Caving boots should provide both ankle support and traction. Top-quality leather hiking or mountaineering boots with Vibram-like

Rubber boots (wellies)

soles (look for white ones that don't scuff up the flowstone) qualify on those counts, but they are expensive and the lug soles will pick up vast quantities of sticky cave mud. And even expensive boots will get beat up in caves by abrasions and repeated soakings. Some outdoor stores carry used boots at a considerable savings. Or you can buy inexpensive hiking boots at discount stores, but they are of poor quality and have an even shorter life span.

Many cavers favor jungle boots with drain holes. Others like combat-type boots found in surplus stores, which are durable and provide excellent ankle support. Still others swear by rubber boots (called "wellies" in England) of the type used in farm work or pouring concrete. They are inexpensive, rotproof, easily patched, and ride

Any leather boot can be given a new life by applying a coat of epoxy or Shoe Goo to the toes, stitches, and sides opposite the instep.

high enough on the leg to be waterproof in shallow water. Look for rubber boots with good fit, tread design (avoid smooth soles), and an inside liner, which provides warmth and makes it easier to insert your feet. Also popular are low-cut rubber boots with steel toes.

One disadvantage of rubber boots is that high water can spill over the tops, making them heavy and uncomfortable. Bending your leg back at the knee will empty most of the water, but not the silt that may have entered. Another disadvantage is that for technical climbing, rubber boots perform poorly compared with good leather hiking boots. Some climbers hike the approach to the cave in leather boots, and then switch to rubber boots for caving.

Your headlamp provides light to plan your next move, but not enough to finish your present move. Designed for the noncarbide caver, the Shoe Light from Clyde's has a bright light in the toe that illuminates your immediate foot placement. Rechargeable batteries and charger are included. Just plug into a household socket or the lighter socket in your car. The estimated battery life is twenty hours per charge.

Socks

For extra insulation and protection, you can wear two pairs of socks. Typically, the inner sock worn is a synthetic blend that wicks moisture away from your feet, and the outer sock is a wool-synthetic blend that adds warmth and support. Some of today's high-tech socks have dense padding at the main contact points and cooling side panels. Thin (1/16-inch) neoprene socks are ideal for wet caves, as they repel water and fit inside boots.

HELMET

No sane and self-respecting caver would ever go subterranean without a hard hat. A helmet offers three main types of protection: from low ceilings and overhangs, from falling rocks, and from falls.

Helmet

People have entered caves wearing all manner of metal, fiberglass, or plastic helmets, mostly mining or construction styles. But the hard hats designed for rock climbers and mountaineers are better at withstanding high impact.

A quality caving helmet should have the following features:

- High-density, impact-absorbing, polyethylene (foam) liner
- Nonstretch nylon chin strap. The helmet is securely held in place by a four-point suspension system—two points on each side— to keep it from sliding off your head. A helmet without a secure chin strap may offer no more protection than a baseball cap. Consider a Velcro quick-arrangement system, and leave it slightly loose—not so loose that the helmet might come off in a fall, but loose enough that you can pull it off in an emergency, such as if it becomes wedged in a crack.
- Mounting bracket for your primary light source. The best types accept both carbide and electric lamps.

Many cavers carry a garbage bag in the liner of the helmet. Weighing almost nothing, it offers a surprising amount of insulation. It can even serve as an emergency bivouac sack— or a trash bag.

LIGHTS

The great debate in caving has long been between carbide and electric lights. Until recently most everyone used carbide lamps, but electric lights, which have become increasingly efficient, safe, and reliable, now dominate the market. Batteries are heavy and bulky, however, and there are still plenty of carbide devotees in the caving community.

Carbide lamps do have some advantages over electric, especially on long trips. For the equivalent light, carbide takes up less room and weighs about half what batteries do. The carbide necessary for twenty to twenty-four hours of light weighs 13 ounces and can be carried in a baby bottle. Water (if it cannot be obtained in the cave) and bottle add another 20 ounces, for a total of about 2 pounds. Alkaline batteries for that same twenty to twenty-four hours would weigh $3^1/2$ pounds.

The other glaring advantage (and potential disadvantage) of carbide is its open flame, which can be used for warmth, cooking, heating water, or fusing rope ends. Cases of hypothermia have been arrested by the warmth of a carbide lamp. In the possession of a careless caver, however, that same flame can start fires and damage ropes.

Whatever your lamp of choice, but especially if you're a carbide caver, get to know your unit. It's essential that you learn how to repair and adjust your lamp. Carry spare parts and know where they go and what they do.

A carbide lamp has two main holding tanks, one for water and one for calcium carbide, a solid chemical. A tube routes the water in controlled drips into the carbide reservoir, producing acetylene gas. The gas is routed into a tube, where it mixes with air and is ignited by a striker. The flame is long and thin, its actual size dependent upon the amount of water dripping into the carbide. A reflector behind the flame focuses the light ahead of the caver, illuminating his path.

To operate a carbide lamp, fill the top reservoir with water and the bottom reservoir one-half to two-thirds full with carbide pebbles. Turn the water-adjustment lever a few clicks clockwise and watch the water as it begins to drip. Let a few drops fall on the chips to prime the carbide, and then tighten the base securely to the top.

Cup your hand over the reflector, covering it as completely as possible, and then draw your hand across the reflector, striking the spark and igniting the gas.

To activate the lamp without priming the carbide, turn the water-adjustment lever all the way clockwise for one or two seconds, then turn it about halfway off and strike the flint.

Carry spare parts for your carbide lamp in a separate container. At the very least, your kit should include the following:

- Two tips
- Two felts
- One gasket
- One flint
- One flint assembly
- One tip cleaner
- One retainer nut
- One flame protector
- One felt holder
- One tool for digging out spent carbide, ideally something dull, such as a Popsicle stick or spoon handle (sharp objects tend to damage the lamp)

Carry extra carbide in a durable, watertight, plastic container, such as a Nalgene bottle or a quality baby bottle. Never carry carbide in a glass container. Carry spare plastic bottles or sturdy Ziploc freezer bags for your spent carbide. Each caver should have his own personal stash of carbide, as assigning it all to one person can cause problems if people are separated. Many cavers choose to carry carbide in plastic baby bottles. The small ones will hold about 8 ounces, enough for three-plus charges. Large bottles ($6^1/2$ inches high) will hold twice that. Other cavers use plastic 35-millimeter film canisters. One charge takes one and a half cans. This permits precise and easy measurement, but it can be time-consuming to fiddle with several small containers.

A caver starting with a full lamp, an extra charge in a spare lamp bottom, and a small baby bottle filled with carbide should have enough to last fifteen to thirty hours of normal use. Substitute a large baby bottle, and you should have twenty-four to forty-eight hours of light.

Always carry carbide out of the cave and dispose of it properly. Leaving it behind poisons wildlife and defaces the cave. Burying it at

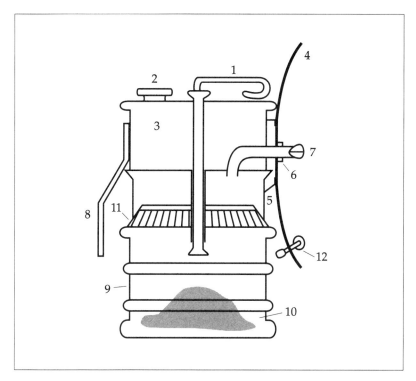

Components of a carbide lamp: 1. Water-adjusting valve. 2. Water filler cap. 3. Water reservoir. 4. Reflector. 5. Reflector-backing plate. 6. Reflector retaining nut. 7. Tip. 8. Mounting blade. 9. Lamp bottom. 10. Carbide chips. 11. Gasket. 12. Flint and striker

the top can be dangerous to cattle and other animals and is likely to anger the landowner. Take it home with you and discard it. Dumping it in an outhouse will help waste decompose.

Be sure your carbide is totally spent before you lock it in a tightly sealed container. Seemingly spent carbide can continue to give off small amounts of acetylene for a while. Trapped in an airtight container, it could build up enough pressure to blow the seal and catch fire. If carbide gets wet, it will produce a cloud of explosive acetylene gas. Even used carbide, not fully depleted, must be kept dry.

Cleaning Carbide Lamps

A common cause of carbide lamp problems is not cleaning them enough. Damp lime clogs parts, corrodes metal, and will eventually set like plaster. After each caving trip, you should at the very least scrape out the sludge and leave the carbide and water chambers open until completely dry.

Every so often, especially if you've had problems with your lamp, you should take it apart and wash it thoroughly inside and out. Scrub all residue from the bottom with an old toothbrush. Remove the filter assembly and clean its parts, scrub the threads, and rinse and flush the tip and water valve. Loosen hard deposits by soaking them in vinegar for a few hours. It may help to run vinegar through the drip mechanism to clear it. After rinsing, air-dry all the parts before reassembling. Replace deteriorating gaskets or filters before they cause problems. For a better seal, lubricate the threads with petroleum jelly.

In between trips, store your lamp in a dry place. If you treat your carbide lamp well, it should work well for many years.

Troubleshooting Carbide Lamps

In order to keep a carbide lamp going and going, you must be an accomplished troubleshooter. As everyone learns very quickly, carbide goes in the bottom, water goes in the top, and acetylene comes out the tip. But let's say you put the water in the top, the carbide in the bottom, then rub your hand across the reflector with your palm on the striker. Nothing happens. Thinking maybe it's a faulty striker, you try a cigarette lighter, and then your friend's already-lit lamp. Nothing.

Return to the basics. There is either no water in the top or no carbide in the bottom, or there is no gas coming out of the tip. The first two are easily checked. Make sure you have filled the bottom with new carbide, not spent carbide or gorp. To check the gas, begin by using your tip cleaner to ream out the tip. If you still can't get a flame, hold your tongue over the tip and try to feel the gas. If you can't feel it, ream out the tip again and retry. Hold the lamp to your ear. With some reflectors, if gas is being emitted, you will hear an oceanlike sound.

If there's still no gas, resist the urge to throttle your lamp and fling it across the cave, causing it to shatter against a speleothem. Try something else, such as checking to make sure the little lever on top is turned on. Now reopen the lamp bottom and check the drip. If there's no water dripping, turn the lever back and forth with one hand while rubbing the drip with the other. This should loosen any sand caught in the line. Water should now flow. If not, you may need professional help.

Here are some basic troubleshooting tips:

- A low flame that diminishes when you open the water valve means the lamp needs water. This is often accompanied by a gurgling at the top.
- A low flame that increases briefly when you open the water valve means the carbide charge is used up.
- A short, crooked flame may indicate a clogged tip.
- A consistently wimpy flame may mean carbide is caked around the water valve. Correct by loosening the bottom and wiggling it. If this fails, check whether the water drips freely. If not, rinse the water tube to remove any dirt. In severe cases of clogging, apply suction to the water tank.
- A "jumpy" flame suggests a wet filter. Change the filter or dry it between layers of clothing, then recharge the lamp. An emergency filter can be rigged from a piece of thick cloth.
- Gas bubbling up through the water suggests either a clogged tip or water turned on too high. If the filter is also wet, you may have a leak between the carbide and water chambers, usually at the joint of the gas tube. If you can locate the leak, you may be able to make a temporary repair with candle wax. To avoid melting the seal, burn the lamp at a low level until a more permanent repair can be made.
- If gas leaks appear around the gasket, the lamp may not be screwed together tightly. It also may have a bad gasket, be badly dented, or have threads heavily caked with deposits. If tightening the stove or replacing the gasket doesn't fix it, try turning the gasket over or adding a second gasket. Clean threads by gouging with the awl of your knife.

Carbide Safety

The most obvious hazard associated with a carbide lamp is the open acetylene flame. Keep such lamps away from highly flammable surroundings, including dusty guano collections or (even the possibility of) explosive gas or fumes. If you smell gas, immediately put out your carbide lamp and exit using an electric light (see "Backup Lights," below). It should be noted that explosive gases, common in coal mines, are rarely found in natural caves. Moreover, carbide lamps almost never explode from excess pressure, as both the tip and the water tube serve as safety valves.

Normally a carbide flame is fairly clean, producing only carbon dioxide and steam. It gives off no carbon monoxide unless burning in oxygen-deficient air, which is rare in caves. Carbide uses much less oxygen and produces much less carbon dioxide than candles or oil lamps. Since a caver doing moderate work exchanges oxygen and carbon dioxide about nine times as often as a carbide lamp does, the flame should be no threat to air quality, even in confined spaces.

Backup Lights

The standard in caving has long been that each caver should carry at least three sources of light. Besides a helmet-mounted lamp, this means two backups, usually a flashlight and a chemical light stick. Many cavers add a candle and matches in a waterproof container for still another backup.

Some cavers carry a complete carbide lamp as a second source. It is an excellent backup, providing additional spare parts. Moreover, it's a headlamp.

When David Bunnell was caving in Borneo, he found that the soot his team's carbide lamps deposited on cave walls and ceilings was greater than usual. They attributed it to inferior carbide. Also, some European-made carbide lamps, which feature a vertical flame, are called "ceiling burners" for their soot-depositing tendencies.

In "My Friend the Carbide Lamp" George Dasher had the following to say about carbide lamp malfunctions:

"There are three methods of communicating with your lamp. One is with silence. This method is used only when the lamp is working perfectly. Few cavers manage silence for very long.

"The second method is to give your carbide lamp a few words of encouragement now and then. These can be muttered under your breath or shouted at the top of your lungs. My suggestion is to shout them at the top of your lungs.

"However, you are far beyond Communication Method Two at this point. You have arrived at Three. Scream, yell, wave your hands. Jump up and down. Pull at your hair. Shout until you feel your eyeballs start to explode from your face. Drool. Use all that language your mother never wanted you to learn. The same effect can be inspired by repeatedly hitting one thumb with a five-pound hammer."

Nevertheless, a flashlight is still the most popular second light. Look for one that is shockproof, is waterproof, and floats in water. Of the larger types, some use D cells and some use C cells. The C cells are smaller and lighter than the Ds, but they die sooner. Look for a flashlight with a recessed push-button switch, which is almost impossible to turn on accidentally. If you use a flashlight with a surface-mounted switch, reverse one of the batteries when not in use so that you won't accidentally drain them.

A popular backup light for caving is the metal Mini Maglite, a diminutive flashlight that uses two AA batteries and a tiny halogen bulb to produce a very bright light. It is small and lightweight, but the high-intensity bulb depletes the batteries in about two hours. The Mini Maglite draws about 300 milliamps of current. But there are imitation Mini Mags that use AAA batteries and draw only half that much, 150 milliamps. Half the energy drain means twice the battery life. It also means less light, but most cavers will hardly notice the difference.

To assure that you can temporarily mount your backup Mini Maglite, you can drill a couple of holes in your helmet and rig a loop of small-diameter shock cord as a strap.

A chemical light stick is a good choice for a backup to the backup. When you're ready to use it, just remove the wrapper, bend it until the inner cylinder breaks, and shake it vigorously. It offers plenty of light for at least sixteen hours. One downside of light sticks is that you can't test them before you use them. Consider carrying two, just in case. Since they lose some juice as they age, put fresh ones in your pack at least every year.

Candles were once the favorite choice for final backup light and are still widely used, but today there are many alternatives. Because long candles are unwieldy and tend to go out when you move around a cave, it's best to cut them down to an inch or so. Be sure to cut the wick out carefully to make lighting easier. Store candles in 35-millimeter film canisters or plastic bags, and keep matches in a waterproof container.

Other popular backup lights include small helmet-mounted electrics, such as the Petzl Micro, and small lights using high-intensity LEDs that can run a week on one battery.

PACKS

Just as there is great diversity in the types of footwear cavers use, there is equal diversity in the packs they employ. Some even choose to leave their packs behind and fill their pockets instead, but one trip through a tight crawlspace is usually enough to convince them of the folly of this strategy.

When choosing a caving pack, consider these variables:

- Versatility. The ideal caving pack allows you as much freedom of movement as possible. It can be worn on different parts of the body—over the shoulders, on the back, or around the waist. Fanny packs offer this sort of versatility.
- Simplicity. The key is how the pack performs while being pushed or dragged through crawlways. A pack with lots of straps, loops, or add-on accessories is bound to snag on pro-

Caver's pack

jections or cracks. Long, narrow packs seem to do best in tight passages.

- Capacity. Choose a pack with the right capacity; for cavers, bigger is not necessarily better. A pack severely underfilled will be limp and difficult to handle. Easiest to move through a cave is a pack that can compress tightly upon its contents, and then expand when pressure subsides.
- Durability. Most packs are made of either nylon/polyester or cotton. Cotton is inexpensive and durable but a nightmare in wet conditions. It soaks up water and will rot if it doesn't dry. Nylon is more expensive but just as strong, more abrasion-resistant, and less absorbent.
- Closure. Most packs rely on zippers, a normally effective seal, but cave mud can quickly immobilize a zipper. A flap with one or two snaps, straps, or buttons tends to leave gaps large enough for gear to escape. The most effective barrier against cave abuse seems to be a flap along with drawstrings.

Surplus stores are good places to look for packs, especially for small canvas bags. Outdoor specialty shops, such as REI and Eastern Mountain Sports, offer high-quality packs at high prices but generally have none designed for caving. See the Resources section at the back of this book for some mail-order outlets that specialize in caving equipment.

Packing the Cave Pack

A favorite packing container of cavers has long been the plastic baby bottle, either without the nipple or with it trimmed to form a gasket beneath the cap. Baby bottles are compact, lightweight, rugged, and watertight. They come in 4- and 8-ounce sizes. An 8-ounce bottle will hold enough carbide for sixteen hours of light; a 4-ouncer might be just perfect for gorp or M&Ms. You can carry spare parts, flashbulbs, even water in baby bottles. Mark the carbide bottle to avoid confusing it with the powdered milk.

If you want to go more high-tech, outdoor stores have high-quality, wide-mouth plastic bottles in all sizes and shapes. Even cheaper, easier, and lighter are Ziploc plastic bags. Freezer bags are the strongest, but don't get mud on the threads or they will never reseal. Items carefully wrapped in multiple bags will generally stay dry, but for a long day of slogging through water, nothing beats plastic bottles.

Other useful packing aids include snap-lid film canisters for spare parts, pieces of foam rubber or Ensolite pad for wrapping cameras, and rubberized bags for survey gear.

Carrying the Cave Pack

Take your pack with you wherever you go in the cave. It's tempting to say, "I'll leave it here while I check out this lead." But half the time, you'll end up dashing madly back to your pack to reload carbide or

Your local hardware store can probably sell you something called "tool dip," a coating that can be applied to your pack, knee pads, and elbow pads to improve durability.

If you're looking to save money, you can construct a pack from two empty plastic jugs. Cut off the bottoms of two large, rectangular plastic containers with handles and glue the containers together. Secure by wrapping bungee cords (the kind with hooks on the end) through the handles. Rig webbing or rope for a carrying strap.

Called a pig by cavers, this plastic pack will slide easily through the mud and rocks. To pull it behind you instead of pushing it, attach another strap around your ankle and clip into the pig strap with a carabiner.

change batteries. Other times, you'll yell back to your companions, "Come on, and bring my pack with you." Do that too many times and you lose the affection of your partners.

Another habit that can grate on your fellow cavers is constantly passing your pack across every obstacle to someone on the other side. It is occasionally easier to pass all the packs through one after another, but some cavers overuse this technique, making others stop and help them when it really isn't necessary. Wrestling your own gear through crawlspaces and over boulders is all part of the rich pageant of caving.

WATER FILTER

Twenty-five years ago, you could drink directly from mountain waterways. Today you run a high risk of contracting a parasitic disease called *giardiasis* (see chapter 8). A good way to defeat this parasite is by filtering the water.

New lightweight water filters eliminate all microorganisms except viruses (some filters even catch those). There are numerous models, some smaller than your water bottle. Filter pores must be 5 microns or smaller to remove *Giardia*. Filters can clog, so make sure the one you buy can be easily cleaned or has a replaceable filter. Water filters are fairly expensive, but they are durable and light-weight.

WATER BOTTLE

Dehydration can be a big problem when you're exercising more than usual. If you're going to carry only a quart or two of water, consider Nalgene wide-mouth, high-density polyethylene bottles. They are bombproof and lightweight. If you have limited access to water sources, you might prefer a collapsible gallon jug, which takes up little room when not filled. Whatever you choose, remember that water weighs more than 2 pounds per quart; carry no more than you need to reach your next water source.

SUNGLASSES

If your approach is surrounded by exposed rock or snow, sunglasses can be a necessity. Even on cloudy days, 60 to 80 percent of ultraviolet (UV) light can reach your unprotected eyes. Reflection off those light-colored surfaces can burn your corneas and cause temporary blindness.

Manufacturers are not required to reveal how much UV protection sunglasses provide, but many do. Look for shades that block 100 percent of UV light and, unless you plan to cross a glacier, transmit 75 to 90 percent of visible light. Polycarbonate (plastic) lenses are lighter, cheaper, and shatterproof. On the other hand, glass is more scratch-resistant, accepts antireflective coatings, and offers greater clarity. Consider photochromic lenses, which darken with increased visible light.

> Lost sunglasses? You can make temporary ones by cutting slits in two pieces of cardboard.

INSECT REPELLENT

This can be an important creature comfort, especially if you're traveling through tick or mosquito country. Repellent won't keep them from buzzing you, but it will prevent them from biting you. A non-aerosol repellent weighs so little, there's no good reason not to take it.

MAP AND COMPASS

If you're traveling through unfamiliar country, a topographic map and compass can be valuable. You can find both at a local backpacking store. Both items are lightweight, so if you're in doubt, you risk little by taking them along. In mountainous areas, where weather fronts can roll in with little warning, a compass can be a lifesaver.

FIRST-AID KIT

At least one member of each caving team should carry a small first-aid kit to treat minor injuries. It should include different-size Band-Aids, butterfly bandages, gauze pads, adhesive tape, disinfectant, and pain medications, such as aspirin. As lightweight as those items are, each member might want to carry a small kit in a waterproof container.

Take along space blankets, which are lightweight and can be used as either ground cloths or coverings. They could be the deciding factor in the battle against hypothermia. Since you can't carry everything that might possibly be needed, leave a more complete first-aid kit, along with spare blankets, water, and food, in the car.

Equipment

Vertical ascents and descents are by far the most hazardous caving maneuvers. For a caver to hang suspended hundreds of feet above a chasm, he must trust his equipment. Nowadays such trust is well placed. Using hardware and techniques adapted from mountaineering, cavers can safely negotiate even the deepest shafts.

ROPES

Modern ropes have come a long way from the horsehair ones used in ancient Carthage or even from the hemp lines used by pre–World War II pioneers in the Alps, where snapped ropes prematurely ended the lives of many climbers. After hemp, climbing ropes were made out of flax, then cotton, followed by manila from the leafstalk of a Philippine tree and sisal from a plant in Yucatán.

During World War II, the U.S. Bureau of Standards concluded that for strength, elasticity, and durability, nylon was superior to all natural fibers. Since 1945, climbing ropes have been fashioned from nylon or Perlon, a trade name for a plastic similar to nylon.

Climbing ropes today are universally kernmantle, German for "jacketed core." A kernmantle rope has a woven nylon sheath over braided continuous fibers of nylon. The sheath holds the core together and protects it against abrasion and ultraviolet radiation. The core strands are laid so that there is virtually no twisting or kinking of the rope. An important quality in a caving rope, it facilitates the long free rappels and prusiks common to the sport. Compared to laid ropes, kernmantle ropes are easier to coil or braid, making them easier to carry and store.

Climbing ropes are usually sold in lengths of 120, 150, 165, and 300 feet, but cavers sometimes need longer or shorter ropes. The choice depends on the depth of the vertical pitches in the caves you intend to explore. If you figure to confront nothing greater than 30-foot pitches, go with the shortest—and therefore lightest—rope you can. On the other hand, extremely long drops sometimes necessitate ropes as long as 1,200 feet or more.

Ropes also come in a variety of thicknesses. For caving use, the recommended diameter is 11 millimeters (7/16 inch). Goldline and Bluewater also come in 9 millimeters (3/8 inch), which is lighter (about 2 pounds per 100 feet) but only slightly more than half as strong as the thicker rope.

Static versus Dynamic Ropes

Another important characteristic to consider when choosing a caving rope is whether it is static or dynamic. It is on this issue that climbers and cavers diverge. Climbers universally favor dynamic ropes, with their greater stretching and shock-absorbing ability. This allows a belayer to stop a falling climber less abruptly, sparing both the rope and the climber's internal organs. Cavers, on the other hand, are seldom run out far from their last anchor point, and a stretchy dynamic rope can be a disadvantage when rappelling or ascending. Ropes designed specifically for caving, such as Bluewater and Pigeon Mountain, are static ropes. They stretch less than 2 percent at low loads and 15 to 20 percent at their breaking points. For dynamic

It's a good idea to mark the midpoint of each climbing rope. That way, if the climber asks how much rope is left, the belayer can answer, for example, "You just passed the halfway mark."

ropes, the low-load stretch is similar, but they elongate by as much as 80 percent before breaking.

Rope Care

Cavers and climbers alike gain confidence by the knowledge that modern ropes do not simply break. They can, however, be cut by abrasion, melted by friction, dissolved by chemicals, or rendered useless by misuse. To prolong the life of your rope, take proper care of it.

Shield the rope from direct sunlight whenever possible. Ultraviolet rays eat away at a rope with the insidiousness of termites undermining a house. Don't hang your rope in the sun; instead, store it in a dark, cool place. Keep stored ropes away from solvents like gasoline, kerosene, and battery acid.

Transport your rope in a rope bag, a glorified stuff sack that has a zipper running its entire length. An inner sleeve allows the bag to expand when you unzip. This is a great way to carry a rope to a cave; it's also an efficient way to feed out a rope from a belay. It eliminates the messy business of having ropes dangling below you that can get tangled in cracks or on projections. The belayer, undistracted by rope management, is free to give her partner the attention he needs.

Keep your rope clean. Never lay a climbing rope in dirt or sand. Never step on a rope. Tiny dirt granules can work their way through the sheath and begin cutting fibers. Once you have approached a cave and are preparing to descend, uncoil your rope atop a backpack, keeping it out of the dirt.

If you do soil your rope, you can wash it in a machine or by hand in a bathtub. Use a mild detergent like Woolite or one made specially for cleaning ropes. Work the soap into the rope. Rinse and hang in a dry, shady place. Do not put the rope in a dryer. Incidentally, a rope is about 15 percent weaker when it's wet. Thus, rigging to avoid water in a cave is a matter of safety, not just comfort.

When using the rope, watch out for sharp edges and projections. You don't ever want anyone in your party hanging on a rope draped nakedly over a sharp edge. If your rope is rubbing against a sharp edge, you must either move the rope or pad the edge. This is most common at or near an anchor point. Remember, the longer the drop

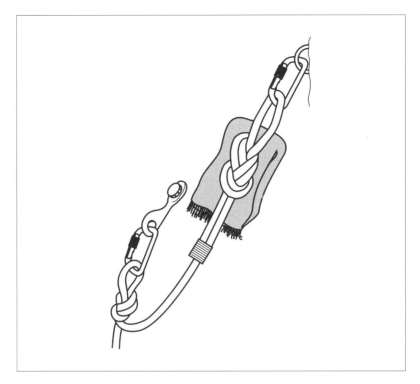

Padding a rope

and the sharper the angle of the rope over the edge, the greater the abrasion potential.

For padding, use a shirt, a belay seat, or whatever is available. Cavers routinely cushion drops with rug pads, homemade leather or canvas, or pieces of garden hose wrapped around the rope. Some favor old denim pant legs, cut open at the seam. Avoid nylon pads, which heat up and melt against a nylon rope. A good pad size is 1 by 3 feet. Attach a 10- to 15-foot length of parachute cord so that the pad can be positioned correctly and tied off.

Inspect your rope often, especially after a fall of any significance. A modern climbing rope has never simply broken from the impact of a fall. So great is the safety cushion built into modern ropes that healthy ones have no chance to break, no matter how severe the fall. The operative word there is *healthy*.

The best way to check a rope for core damage is to pinch a tiny loop of it. If it pinches flat, the core is damaged and the rope should be replaced. If you can't pinch it flat—that is, there is still a hole in the loop big enough for your finger—the rope is okay. You should perform a thorough check on every inch of it before every trip or at least once a week. It's time-consuming but well worth the effort. The worst piece of equipment a caver can have is a damaged rope.

> Some caving teams test a rope by tying it off and having four or more people pull on it.

Since you are hanging life and limb on your rope, it makes sense to listen to what the experts say about when to stop climbing on it. David McClurg of the National Speleological Society recommends retiring a rope from critical use after three or four heavy caving seasons. And says Chris Gore, technical consultant for Beal ropes, "Any rope suffering a long fall of great severity should be retired immediately."

To get the longest and best performance from your ropes, handle them properly during use, pad them against abrasion, wash them before they get too dirty, and store them out of the sunlight and away from harmful chemicals.

HARNESS

Once upon a time, cavers and climbers tied their climbing ropes directly to their waists. But an arrested fall with a rope tied to your waist can yank your spleen up into your throat, and aren't you glad those days are past? Today most cavers link their ascending and descending devices to a sit-harness, made from pieces of wide (1- or 2-inch) nylon tape sewn together.

Using a harness has several advantages over tying directly to the waist. It's a more convenient way to join rope and torso, and it provides loops for clipping on runners and other gear. Most important,

There are lots of ways to clean your rope, some more effective than others. You can hang it in a waterfall, tow it behind a boat, or float it down some rapids. You can wash it in a washing machine, and Bob & Bob sells a rope washer that works off a garden hose.

But all of those methods have drawbacks. Streams carry grit, which can penetrate the rope and abrade the fibers. Bob & Bob's rope washer is ineffective with low water pressure, and intricate coiling and rearranging is necessary to wash a rope in a machine.

But here's a simple, low-tech method that caver Chuck Porter shared with his readers in the *Northeastern Caver.* It requires a bathtub and two plastic scrub brushes. Fill the tub half full with warm water and add mild soap, such as Ivory flakes. Submerge the dirty rope in a loose coil. Then make a "rope sandwich," placing the rope between the bristles of the two brushes. Slide the brushes back and forth along the rope. Start at one end and work your way to the other end. It doesn't take long.

in the event of an arrested fall, a harness distributes the impact force over a wider area of the body.

A good harness is fail-safe—that is, if one part fails, another part takes up the weight. It is also comfortable, versatile, easy to put on and take off, and has convenient-to-check buckles, knots, or seams. Sewing is the strongest and most comfortable way to join webbing.

Take proper care of your harness. Read and follow all instructions carefully. Keep the harness away from caustic substances, such as battery acid or gasoline. Even more than rope, it is susceptible to ultraviolet damage, so be sure to inspect your harness regularly.

CARABINERS
Affectionately known as krabs or biners (pronounced "beaners"), carabiners are steel or aluminum alloy snap-links that work like giant

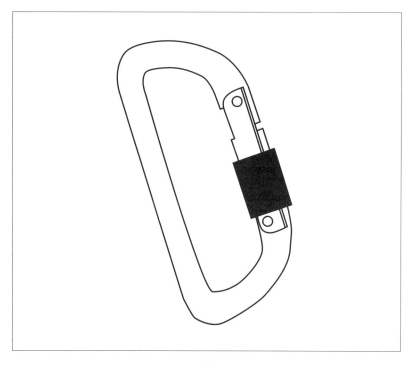

Carabiner

safety pins. They allow you to attach a rope to the anchor you sling or place in the rock. They are also used for rappelling, attaching to a belay or safety line, lowering gear, and attaching gear to a pack.

They come in two basic shapes: oval and D. The D shape is stronger, opens more easily when weighted, and permits a smoother flow of rope.

A carabiner has a spring-loaded gate that opens inward to accept rope or runner and snaps closed when pressure is released from the gate. Standard-gate carabiners allow you to open the gate with one thumb, an important convenience when you're fiddling with equipment in a deep pit. But cavers, who seldom clip dozens of carabiners, tend to prefer the security of locking carabiners. Locking carabiners screw shut on exposed threads or on an internal pin in the sleeve housing.

If you are concerned that a carabiner might open at the wrong time, use two simultaneous carabiners, positioning them so that the gates open in opposite directions. Or use a screw-gate carabiner. Once a screw-gate is locked, it will come unlocked only when you want it to. You might be tempted to use screw-gates everywhere you use a carabiner, but it's really unnecessary. Standard-gate biners can open only if the gate strikes a projection at just the right angle. You don't normally need that extra security, and it's time-consuming to lock multiple biners.

If carabiners are used properly—they are designed to be weighted lengthwise—they are exceptionally strong. The minimum breaking strength is 2,500 pounds, and some reach 5,000 pounds, but only if the carabiner is weighted along the major axis. Don't ever set up a biner so that the pull is straight out from the gate, for then the breaking strength is no greater than the gate pin—usually less than 500 pounds.

Cavers tend to need fewer carabiners than climbers. Those who use the Frog rigging system typically need two on the cow's tail and one to attach to the seat harness. Use locking types for the main rigging and for clipping into your harness, or alternatively, use maillons, which are smaller, lighter, and have no hinged gates.

Carabiner Care

Most carabiners are made of aircraft-quality aluminum alloy, with a life expectancy of at least ten years. Still, it is important to inspect biners periodically for disqualifying cracks. Corrosion can eat away at them, leaving a fine white powder. This is especially a problem in humid caves. If you have any doubts about a carabiner's viability, discard it. The expression "Better safe than sorry" has no greater applicability than in caving equipment.

Here are some tips for loving care of your carabiners:

- Keep them away from alkalies, which will ravage the alloy.
- Rinse them in fresh water if they get near salt water. Even sea spray will rapidly corrode aluminum alloy.
- Lubricate the gates with a silicone-based spray if the action becomes rough.

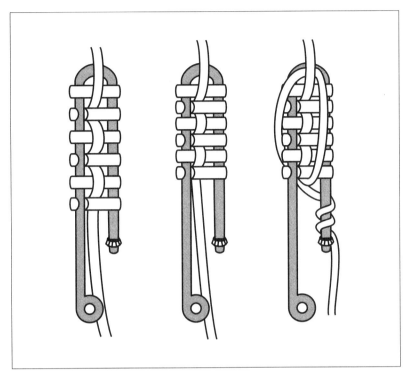

Rack descender

- Don't drop or throw carabiners long distances; the impact can cause fractures in the metal.
- Don't put a three-way pull on carabiners; they are designed for a two-way pull only.

DESCENDERS

Used for rappelling fixed ropes, these devices permit a controlled slide by creating friction. The original technique was the *Dulfursitz,* also called the *body rappel,* a way of wrapping the rope around your body to create enough friction to slow your descent.

The body rappel has been out of favor for many years. In its place, we have the bobbin, the rappel rack, and the figure-eight. The bobbin, long the standard in Europe, is growing in popularity in the United States.

The rappel rack comes in a number of variations, all of which work by bending the rope around alternate sides of metal bars threaded onto a long, U-shaped rack. Thread the rope as shown. Maintain control by gripping the rope below the rack. Slide the bars up the rack to trap the rope. By pulling the rope over the rack top and wedging it between the rack and the exit rope, you achieve what's called a soft-lock. By looping the rope through the carabiner and back over the rack top, you complete a hard-lock. Safe use of the rack requires practice. As with all caving equipment, gain familiarity aboveground before you have to depend on it in a cave.

To rig the figure-eight, thread the rappel rope through the big hole, then around behind the little hole, and clip to a locking biner. Clip another locking carabiner (or two regular biners, gates reversed)

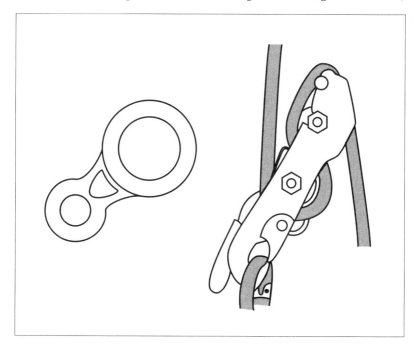

Figure-eight and bobbin descender

on your harness through the small hole. The friction created by this bend will allow a capable rappeller to control speed of descent. The disadvantage of the figure-eight is that it tends to put kinks in the rope. And as the rope is dragged against an edge, it can form a ring knot. To counter this, use a figure-eight with ears, or projections.

BOLTS

Bolts are a protection of last resort. If you take the time and trouble to put in a bolt, make sure it is bombproof. It should be solid, stainless steel, and deep. Most experienced cavers use bolts only when doing new, vertical exploration with no available natural anchors.

PITONS

Also called pins or pegs, pitons are chrome-molybdenum ("chrome-moly") steel spikes that climbers hammer into cracks to secure anchors. Piton shapes and sizes vary, but all have an eyelet through which a carabiner or piece of webbing can be attached, and all damage the rock. Today, conscientious cavers use pitons only as a last resort, when they cannot place a chock or a spring-loaded camming device (SLCD) in a crack.

Despite their disadvantages, pitons persist. They are still manufactured in this country, most successfully by Black Diamond, and caving routes exist that require pitons, most notably in Hawaii when rigging lava-tube drops. The types of pitons used most often by cavers are medium-size angles and horizontal blade pitons.

Lost Arrow, or horizontal, pitons (modeled after the original John Salathé design) are usually 2 to 6 inches long and suitable for $1/8$- to $3/8$-inch cracks.

The next size larger, angle pitons, are pieces of metal bent into U-shaped channels to provide three points of contact with the rock, at the back and the two edges of the channel. They are big but hollow, and therefore light. They fit cracks from $1/2$ to $11/2$ inches in width. The smallest angles—$1/2$-inch and $5/8$-inch—are called *baby angles*. The $3/4$-inch angle is called a *standard*, or *regular*. And the larger ones—1-inch, $11/4$-inch, and $11/2$-inch angles—are referred to by their size, as in "Send down a 1-inch angle."

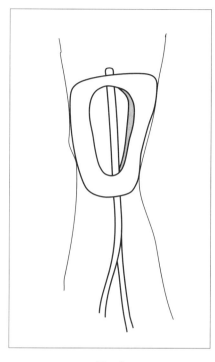

Chock

CHOCKS

Variously known as *chockstones, nuts, stoppers, wedges, tapers,* or *hexentrics,* chocks are used more for underground lead climbs than for rigging. They are pieces of metal of various sizes and shapes, strung with cable or rope, that fit into irregularities in the rock. Imagine fitting a pebble into a crack, tying a piece of rope around that pebble, and giving it a downward tug. The stone will stop as the crack pinches or bottlenecks.

Chocks come in two basic shapes: tapers and hexentrics. *Tapers,* also known as wedges or stoppers, are rectangular with sloping sides. They are perfect for flaring cracks that narrow in the back. Some tapers are offset, with no parallel sides, and using them at different angles effectively produces different sizes. Be aware, though, that offsets are less reliable in marginal placements.

Tapers range from thumbnail-size micros strung with wire the diameter of dental floss to beefy 1½-inch nuts tied with Spectra cord, reputed to be stronger than steel of the same size.

Cable has replaced rope for all but the largest tapers. Not only is it stronger than rope (and usually stronger than the nut itself), but it's also stiff, which allows a few extra inches of reach, often the difference between placing and not placing the protection. If a chock fails, it is almost certainly due to poor placement and not a broken cable. With extended use, however, the cable can fray beneath the head of the nut; if so, it's time to replace it.

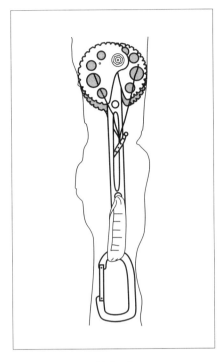

Friend

Hexentrics, or hexes, are six-sided chocks that excel in cracks up to $3^1/2$ inches. Placed endwise, the hex is slotted in the crack like a big taper. For a bottleneck placement, nothing beats a big hex.

SPRING-LOADED CAMMING DEVICES

The spring-loaded camming device is undoubtedly the protection most commonly used today. Developed in the seventies and marketed as the Friend by Ray Jardine in 1978, the SLCD has revolutionized climbing and caving.

SLCDs have three or four pear-shaped lobes that are attached to an axis and controlled by a trigger. When you squeeze the trigger, it causes the device to retract, thereby becoming smaller. Keeping the trigger squeezed, a climber places the SLCD in a crack and releases the trigger, causing the cams to spring back into shape. As the SLCD expands, it grips the inside of the crack. Putting weight on that device merely causes it to tighten its grip.

Friends, easy to place, easy to remove, and bombproof, were considered cheating by some climbers of the old school. Others thought they sounded too good to be true. But they turned out to be as reliable as their reputation. They do no damage to the rock and have opened up areas of caves that once seemed unprotectable, benefits that soon won over the skeptics. Today there is little or no vocal opposition to SLCDs.

SLCDs really show their strength in parallel-sided cracks, which are unsuitable for nuts. They are also excellent in loose rock and around expanding flakes. An expanding flake is a flake so thin that when pressure is applied, it appears to move. If you attack an expanding flake with a piton, the crack expands with the flake's movement and spits out the piton. A camming device, on the other hand, expands to fill the crack, preventing a fall.

SLCDs come in a wide range of sizes and can fit cracks from $1/2$ inch to 9 inches wide. Since the introduction of the Friend, there have been many SLCD copycats, as well as some significant improvements. Brand names include Camalots, Aliens, TCU (Three-Cam Units), and Wired Bliss.

ETRIERS

Also called *aiders, aid slings,* and *aid ladders,* etriers are made of 1-inch flat webbing (as opposed to tubular webbing) tied to create a ladder in which you can stand. Cavers mostly use etriers to get over a nasty lip at the top of a pit. It's usually a case where the bend is so sharp and the caver is so tight against the lip that he can't slide his ascenders up. The caver will sometimes counter this by rigging an etrier, which allows him to take weight off the rope and slide up.

Etriers range from three to five rungs; which you choose may be governed by your height. In either case, they are small and lightweight. They used to be made of wooden rungs threaded onto rope. Later, aluminum replaced the wood. That made the ladder lighter, but it still didn't pack well. Etriers made of webbing, on the other hand, can be wadded up and stuffed into packs. Although it might seem easier to place a boot on a metal rung, a little practice is all that is needed to feel comfortable standing in webbing.

CABLE LADDERS

Lightweight cable ladders are made of two parallel stainless-steel cables with metal rungs held in place by metal ferrules crimped to the cables. These longtime caving favorites are still used today, mostly for "nuisance drops" of 30 feet or less. Ladders make it possible to move a group up or down quickly. Even with a ladder, you should usually use a rope for belay rather than trusting it alone.

ASCENDERS

A rope ascender is a clamp—a mechanical hand, really—that grips a rope without ever letting go or getting tired. It was invented in the fifties by Swiss bird-watchers who needed an easier way to climb trees. Today ascenders are a central piece of equipment for vertical cavers. They're also used in the hauling system—a downward-pointing ascender anchored to the rock prevents haul bags from sliding back down.

Working on a ratchet principle, ascenders slide up a rope, but when weighted, a cam causes the handle to pinch the rope and stop downward movement. This does minimal damage to the rope, although if you were to use mechanical ascenders over and over on the same rope, it would eventually fray. Realistically, however, ropes wear out for other reasons before that happens.

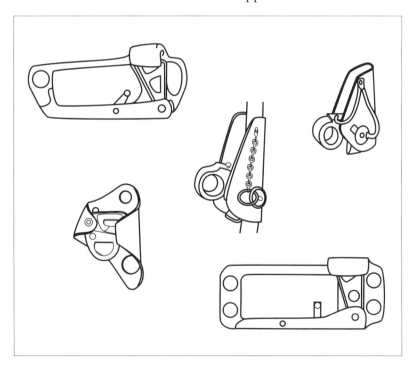

Ascenders. Clockwise from top left: Jumar, Gibbs, CMI, Croll. Center: Gibbs.

Jumar is a brand name for one particular type of ascender (others include Gibbs, Petzl, CMI, and CLOG), but it has become synonymous in the climbing community with the act itself. It's common for climbers to say, "I jumared up to the first ledge," even if they are using a competing brand. Climbers prefer the Jumar ascender because it can be clipped to a rope without taking it apart. The disadvantages of a Jumar are that it tends to slip on icy ropes and wears out more quickly, especially on muddy caving ropes.

Cavers usually prefer a Gibbs ascender for long freefall drops. It doesn't wear out as fast, and you don't have to use your hands to move it up

Caver in ascender

the rope. When rebelaying, however, it has the disadvantage of having to be taken apart over and over, which raises the risk that you will drop part of it.

The original ascender—the prusik knot—is still used today, especially for shorter drops where rigging mechanical ascenders is too much trouble, or when backpacking needs call for lightweight prusik slings instead of heavy Jumars or Gibbses.

BELAY DEVICES

To belay is to pay out rope to the leader from a secure position. As a caver is placing protection, the belayer should be smoothly feeding out rope, maintaining enough slack to avoid pulling the leader off the rock. If the leader falls, the belayer has to make sure no more rope feeds out.

In the past twenty years or so, the body belay has been replaced by several devices designed to enhance that friction without sacrificing human skin. The first was the Sticht plate, a 4-ounce disk with a hole in it. A bight of rope is passed through the hole and clipped to a screw-gate carabiner on the harness. During belay, the rope passes through the belay plate, through the carabiner, then back through the belay plate again. The belayer's hands do exactly what they would do during a body belay. The radical bend that the rope makes as it passes through the belay plate creates the friction necessary to hold a fall.

Another device that can be used for belaying is a figure-eight ring, so called because it looks like the numeral 8. The goal of increasing friction is the same as for the Sticht plate: The rope is threaded through the bigger hole of the figure-eight ring, then back through the smaller hole; then it's clipped to a locking carabiner on the climber's harness. The radical turn of the rope creates the friction necessary to control the rope.

All belay devices are attached to the belayer with a locking carabiner.

WEBBING

Nylon straps known as *webbing* come in two basic styles and have countless uses. One style is the 1-inch tubular webbing used to make runners. Runners are loops of webbing approximately 6 feet long tied with a water knot. They have many different purposes, one of the most important of which is to control the way the rope runs. To avoid rope drag—excessive resistance—you want the rope running more or less straight, not zigzagging all over the rock. Runners can help you achieve that. Or you might use runners to move the rope away from trouble spots like sharp edges or waterfalls.

If you wanted to use a tree for protection, you might girth-hitch it with a runner. You also could use a runner to tie several anchors together, to equalize anchor points so that you're stressing several instead of just one, or to carry gear slung over your shoulder.

The other type of webbing, called *tie-off loops* or *hero loops*, are short loops about 2 feet long made of 1/2-inch or 9/16-inch tubular webbing and tied with a water knot. If you are unable to drive a piton

VERTICAL EQUIPMENT REQUIRED FOR BEGINNERS

For horizontal caves with no pits, carry a caver's sling, which consists of 20 feet of 1-inch webbing and a carabiner.

For intermediate caves with small (25- to 30-foot) drops, carry the following:

- One 50-foot 9-millimeter handline
- Descender
- Caver's sling and locking carabiner
- Prusik slings
- $^9/_{16}$-inch webbing ladder (etrier)
- Safety loop (20-inch diameter) of 7-millimeter Perlon,

in all the way, you might girth-hitch webbing around the piton close to the rock to reduce leverage. Known as "tying off a piton," this relocates the pressure point closer to the rock. A hero loop can also be threaded through the eye of a piton, then clipped to the carabiner through which the rope passes. This gives the rope more flexibility.

PULLEYS

Vertical caving groups should have at least two pulleys in their possession. They are especially valuable for hauling large amounts of gear and for rescue operations. One of the best is called a Rock Exotica, which has a built-in cam to prevent the load from sliding back down the rock. Most modern pulleys employ a ball-bearing system for a smoother haul. It's a good idea to carry a spare pulley in case you drop one. If that happens, don't forget to yell, "Rock!"—the monosyllabic signal that something has been dropped.

5

Moving through Caves

The passages traveled by most cavers are horizontal or nearly so, although they are often connected by pits and drops. The techniques necessary to negotiate moderate passages come naturally to us, and have since we were kids. They include walking, scrambling, traversing, stooping, and crawling.

WALKING

Walking is the preferred mode of travel whenever possible. In wide-open caverns, you can walk upright. When ceiling height is not an issue, you can focus most of your attention on where to place your feet. Walking in a cave has been compared to hiking cross-country. You may have to climb hillocks, scamper over boulders, cross or follow streams, or scale rock faces. On rough terrain, it's wise to test your foot placements before applying your full weight.

SCRAMBLING

Scrambling is the technique you use when a passage is too steep to walk up but not steep enough to demand classic rock-climbing skills. It may include walking, sliding, climbing, slithering, or any combination thereof. The hands are mostly used for balance, and the legs support most of the weight. Generally, a cave passage that slopes less than 45 or 50 degrees can be scrambled.

Although few scramblers use a belay line, many more should. Consider not only the difficulty of the terrain but also the possibility and ramifications of a serious fall. Except on the most moderate slopes, descent is usually more difficult than ascent, because it's harder to see the next holds. Whether going up or down, your goal is to maintain three points of contact with the rock until the fourth is secure on a new hold. In scrambling, those contact points may include hands, feet, stomach, back, buttocks, arms, legs, or even your helmeted head.

Always look before you step, just as you would aboveground. Don't jump or lunge. Plan ahead by shining your light two or three steps in front and letting your feet follow. Don't try to sightsee on the move. If the terrain is steep, you will feel more secure facing the rock. Beginners who try to descend facing outward may find that though this can be faster outdoors in the right terrain, it is seldom worth the risk in a dark cave. Remember, cavers have to rely on wet, slippery holds much more than climbers.

Scrambling is an easy technique to practice outdoors. Seek out rocky terrain with topographical variety. Scrambling over large boulders is a realistic simulation of what you will have to do in many caves.

Avoid scrambling through areas rich in speleothems. Use a rope or go around.

TRAVERSING

Traversing is moving sideways, usually to skirt some obstacle in the way. For example, facing a passage with a steep drop, followed by a rise, your party may decide it's quicker to traverse around the side of the minicanyon, avoiding the steep drop and the stream below. Often you will have to face the wall and shuffle your feet rather than cross them, settling them carefully on holds before looking ahead for the next solid placement.

When the traverse is particularly dangerous or difficult, cavers should be belayed, ideally from both sides to prevent a pendulum fall. The first caver, who will have only a single belay, should be the most accomplished climber in the party. If many people must pass a difficult stretch, rig a safety line that is anchored securely at both the start and finish.

STOOPING

In most caves, you're never far from a restrictive passageway. In those 4 feet high or more, most cavers choose to stay on their feet and bend over. If the distance is great, however, this stoop-walk tires the back. Try resting your hands on your thighs, which helps support the upper body.

When the passage floor becomes slippery, unstable, or steep, progress becomes more arduous. You may need to steady yourself by

Methods of moving through a cave

placing your hands on the walls or ceiling, but as always, take care not to damage any delicate formations. For the sake of both you and the cave, plan ahead to determine where to place hands and feet.

As the passage diminishes in height, you will have to adapt your stoop-walk to the conditions. At first you can extend one leg behind the other and shuffle, keeping your weight over your feet. Push off the rear foot and use the hands for balance when you can. For a time, you will be able to squat on your haunches in kind of a duckwalk.

CRAWLING

At some point, as a passage shrinks to 2 to 4 feet high, you will have to leave your feet and crawl. Most people think of crawling as a hands-and-knees maneuver, but several variations are available to you. Anybody who has given a kid a horsey-back ride knows that the kneecaps are a fragile, easily stressed part of the human anatomy. If you expect to do extensive crawling, wear knee pads.

Get relief by periodically shifting your weight from hands and knees to elbows and toes, and then to forearms and ankles. At times you may want to crawl on your side, pushing with the feet and legs and pulling with the arms. Alternate these methods to avoid stressing any one area of your body.

When the passage shrinks further—say to 10 to 24 inches high—you must crawl on your belly like a reptile, pushing your pack ahead. In some cases you may have to remove your helmet and push that ahead as well. Sometimes the first caver through can crawl back and help the others with their packs and helmets. By retreating feet-first, the lead caver can sometimes loop pack straps around his ankle and pull them through.

Study the shape of the squeeze and plan the best way to guide your body through it. If your shoulders are your biggest problem, you may have to narrow them by extending one arm ahead and dragging the other by your side. You lose pulling power this way, but it may be your only choice. Remember to stay relaxed and pliable. Panic is your worst enemy.

As long as the passage is wide enough to allow your elbows to splay out and return to the sides of your body, crawling is relatively easy and stress-free; after all, it's a maneuver you mastered when you were only a few months old. You will progress by wriggling your body, wormlike, while pressing your hands and feet against nubbins and dishes in the cave floor. Look for any irregularity that will provide a purchase. Although the hands help to pull the caver forward, the stronger leg muscles should do most of the work.

Most people have physical or psychological trouble when the ceiling is less than 12 inches high. The smallest passageway most cavers can negotiate varies between $7^1/_2$ and 12 inches. It's often said that if the helmet can fit through a squeeze, so can the climber. But this isn't always true, as many helmets are only 7 or 8 inches high. What is usually true is that if your upturned boot can make it, so can you.

Determine early on how small a hole you can fit through—you may be amazed. If the shoulders, chest, and hips make it, the rest of your body will too. Don't forget to empty your pockets.

If you are trying to squeeze through a passage that is just wide enough, success depends in large part on your ability to relax, exhale, and push off with your feet. By letting out your breath completely, you can reduce your chest measurement by $1/_2$ to 1 inch. When trying to squeeze through the minimum space, exhale completely, shove with all your might, take a small breath, and then let it out and shove again.

Even a tiny purchase can allow you a straight-leg push powerful enough to overcome significant pressure on your chest and pelvis, popping you out the other side. Lacking that purchase, a following caver can sometimes provide a hand or foot as a foothold for another.

CONSERVING ENERGY

Whatever techniques you use for maneuvering your body through a cave, your ultimate goals remain the same: to move safely and conserve energy that you may need to complete the trip. You can conserve energy by moving efficiently, resting muscles not in use, eating right, and fine-tuning your body through training.

Move Efficiently

After you've read this section and understand the basics of moving efficiently, practice the techniques on the surface before going under-

ground. Seek out trails and cross-country routes where you can practice efficient movement on taxing terrain. When you go caving, carry
those techniques over to the approach and then into the cave itself.

The following are some suggestions for maximizing your efficiency:

- *Stay balanced.* This has to do with agility and foot placement,
  but it also has to do with load distribution. Say you are moving in a crouch through a low passage with your arms swinging naturally at your sides. Bent over, pack on your back, you
  feel unbalanced. But you find you can right yourself by
  swinging your pack over your buttocks and holding the
  straps in your hands locked together behind your back. This
  redistributes the weight from your upper body to your hips,
  with a remarkable saving of energy.

  Indeed, your pack can be a handy counterweight in your
  balancing act. Experiment on the surface by climbing steep
  hills and noting how the relocation of your pack helps or hin-
  ders your progress. In caves, though, you generally shouldn't
  take your pack off except in the tightest passages.

  Some cavers add counterweights to their hard hats to balance the weight of their lamps. Another trick is to equalize a
  load, with an equal weight, such as a coiled rope, on both
  sides of your body.

- *Keep your head up.* Whether you're moving through immense
  galleries or pinched passages, hold your head as high as possible. It will improve your posture and permit you to move
  briskly. In a passage 4 feet high, for example, you can either
  crawl or crouch. Choose the crouch, keeping your head as
  close to the ceiling as possible. You may hit rock, but that's
  why you're wearing the helmet. After a few blows, your aim
  will improve. If you never hit the ceiling, you are probably
  moving with your head too low. Exception: In low passages
  where speleothems line the ceiling, stay well below them.

  In some crawlways, there is a channel or groove in the ceiling. By keeping your head up in that groove, you may be able
  to crouch or bear-walk instead of crawl. Don't be afraid to

take off your helmet if it makes it significantly easier to move. Removing loose pebbles from the floor of a crawlway is easy to do and saves wear and tear on body and clothes.

- *Stay level.* Say you enter a room in a cave and face several route choices. All other things being equal, choose the one that demands the least change in altitude. Eyeball a line to where you want to go, and try to stay on that level. The most level route may be circuitous or take you over breakdown, but it probably will drain less energy from your reserves than the up-and-down route. If you encounter a rock, step over or around it rather than using it as a stepping-stone. That micro-ascent and descent taxes your precious energy.

- *Pay attention to your surroundings.* The fewer wrong moves you make and wrong turns you take, the less energy you expend. Watch the caver in front of you. Her lamp illuminates an area farther ahead of your position. If she has trouble, learn from her experience.

  Turn around often and imagine how the passage will look on the way out. This is especially important at route junctions. Passages often look entirely different from the opposite perspective.

Some cavers have said that the first time they really saw a cave was when they were on a photographic or surveying party. The slower pace and the necessary attention to detail allowed them to exercise their powers of observation. For others, getting lost was the catalyst for sharpening their senses.

- *Use energy-saving free-climbing techniques.* Accomplished rock climbers seem to flow up the rock in one continuous liquid movement. Many of their moves pit one group of muscles in opposition to another group, which demands less energy than relying on sheer brute strength. Techniques such as layback-ing and chimneying (see chapter 6) use this opposition theory, allowing you to steady and brace yourself (and rest key muscles) when the handholds are skimpy or absent. For example, you may be able to cross a ledge by pressing your fingers against the ceiling in opposition to your feet on the ledge.

Rest Intelligently

Every chance you get, isolate and relax the muscles not in use. Techniques such as yoga and meditation, learned and practiced aboveground, will make this easier.

Both on the approach and in the cave, it's better to slow your pace and keep going than to take frequent stops. Once you're committed to a rest stop, however, make the most of it. Sitting takes less effort than standing, and lying down less effort still. Elevate the legs above the torso and close your eyes. But don't rest too long, or those muscles will chill out and stiffen.

Eat and Drink Right

Energy is calories, and for maximum energy, carbohydrates are in, fats and proteins are out. Fat is an important long-term energy source, but the average American has already stored way more than he needs. Nearly 40 percent of the average American's calories are derived from fat. Try to cut your fat tally to below 30 percent of your total calories. The new FDA-mandated food labels make this an easy calculation.

When caving, emphasize carbohydrates even more than usual. Carbs, which include both simple and complex sugars (starches), are quickly digested and converted to energy. Fats and proteins take longer to digest.

It used to be that cavers and other endurance athletes would reach for a candy bar whenever energy flagged, but we now know that flooding the system with simple sugars causes a rapid boost in energy followed by a precipitous drop. It's better to eat light, frequent snacks with plenty of complex carbohydrates. Good cave foods include bagels, unleavened bread, dried and fresh fruit, gorp, and sports bars, which are higher in complex carbohydrates than candy bars. Some cavers make their own trail mix and keep it handy for easy access.

There's nothing like a cold beer after a workout, right? Wrong. It is thirst-quenching in the short run, but alcohol actually dehydrates the body, stimulating the kidneys to pass more water than is being consumed. In excess, it shreds concentration and dulls insights. Alcohol has no place in caves. Leave it in the ice chest back in the car.

Although it has no calories, water is even more important for efficient performance than food. We humans are veritable reservoirs of water. The brain is cushioned by fluid, joints are lubricated by fluid, blood is 90 percent water, and every biochemical reaction requires water. Under normal conditions, humans can survive for about three weeks without food but for only three days without water.

Make a conscientious effort to drink often and regularly. Drink before you are thirsty, because you know you should. Drink as much water in cool caves as you do in the hot outside. As your effort increases, so does your need for water. Exercise causes water loss through sweating, breathing, and metabolism. If it is not replaced, a fluid deficit results. With only a 2 percent deficit, we experience mental deterioration, nausea, loss of appetite and energy, an increased pulse rate, and a 25 percent loss in efficiency. A 12 percent fluid deficit causes a swollen tongue, inability to swallow, sunken eyes, and neurological problems. A fluid deficit of 15 percent is potentially lethal.

Dehydration is the cause or a complication of many wilderness ailments. It contributes to hypothermia, heat illness, altitude sickness, and frostbite. It worsens fatigue, decreases the ability to exercise, and reduces alertness. End-of-the-day headache, weariness, and irritability are often preliminary signs of dehydration.

Stay Fit

The best energy saver a caver can have is a fit body. Fitness is the ability to do work with reasonable efficiency and without undue fatigue. Adequate fitness often makes the difference between fun and misery. A caver's fitness should be sufficient not only for normal caving activities, but for possible emergencies as well.

Physical fitness has four components:
- *Cardiorespiratory endurance.* This is the sustained ability of your heart and blood vessels to carry oxygen to your body's cells.
- *Muscular fitness.* This consists of both strength, the force a muscle produces in one effort, and endurance, the ability to perform repeated muscular contractions in quick succession.
- *Flexibility.* This is the ability of your joints to move freely and without discomfort through their full range of motion.
- *Body composition.* This refers to how much of your weight is lean mass (muscle and bone) and how much is fat.

Fitness needs to be specific to the tasks you wish to perform. Judging fitness on the basis of bulging muscles or the ability to run a six-minute mile misses the point for cavers. Although *aerobic* exercise

Make intelligent food choices for in-cave meals and snacks. Include the following:
- Quick-energy foods high in complex carbohydrates.
- Foods that require no refrigeration or cooking.
- Foods that are simple and unmessy. When a caver is covered in mud, "finger-lickin'" chicken doesn't cut it.
- Foods that are palatable. The carb-versus-fat debate has no meaning if the food goes uneaten.
- Foods that can be eaten as several snacks throughout the day, especially if the trip is long.
- More foods than you think you need. Trips tend to take longer than expected, and food may be an important weapon in the battle against hypothermia.
- Foods packaged to withstand abuse and moisture. Airtight plastic containers, such as baby bottles, Nalgene, and Tupperwear, are effective. For more durable goods, use Ziploc plastic bags, which take up less room in your pack.

(a continuous, rhythmic exercise during which the body's oxygen needs are still being met) boosts cardiorespiratory fitness and is important for general health, it is not essential for most caving activities, which tend to be *anaerobic* (exercise at an intensity level that exceeds the ability of the body to dispose of the lactic acid produced by the muscles). On the other hand, a high level of cardiorespiratory fitness will help you on long, hilly approaches, long rope climbs, and occasionally on sustained scrambles inside caves.

Other things you can do to improve fitness for caving include weight training, stretching, and watching your weight.

Weight Training. Weight training can be of value to everyone, not just those interested in becoming bodybuilders. Caving places demands on a wide range of muscle groups. Paired with regular aerobic exercise, weight training improves strength and muscle endurance and creates an overall feeling of fitness. Bicycling develops one set of muscles, running another, but weight training works out a whole range of muscles likely to be used by an ambitious caver.

The guiding principle of any sort of muscle development is that of overload: contracting a muscle group against more and more resistance. The overload exerted on the muscle is increased a step at a time—a technique called *progressive resistance*—so that it continues to develop.

Lifting light to moderate weights (50 to 75 percent of the maximum amount you can lift) with many repetitions builds muscle endurance—that is, the ability to contract a muscle repeatedly in quick succession, as in lifting twenty mail sacks in two minutes. This type of training can enhance oxygen utilization by muscle cells and improve endurance.

Higher resistance (more than 75 percent of your maximal lift) with fewer repetitions primarily increases muscle strength and size. Strength is the force a muscle produces in one all-out effort, as when you swing a pick into concrete.

Using small weights lets you work isolated muscles better than calisthenics, such as push-ups, that rely on body weight alone. A typical workout with weights includes a warmup of five to ten minutes followed by an exercise routine that leaves the muscles thoroughly exhausted. Your exact routine should be crafted with a trainer, a specialist who can tell you just how to position yourself, how to lift so as to prevent strain or injury, which weights or machines to use, and how many repetitions and sets to do.

A good weight-training routine for overall fitness consists of about a dozen exercises—six for the upper body and six for the lower. Schedule your workouts so that each muscle has a full day's rest before you exercise it again. If you exercise the same muscle two days in a row, it won't have a chance to recuperate amd will become weaker, not stronger.

Here are some strength-training tips:
- Warm up. A five- to ten-minute warmup increases blood flow and helps prevent soreness and strains in muscles, tendons, and ligaments.
- Work larger muscles first. The large muscles of the legs, chest, and back require heavier loads to achieve results. It's best to target them first before fatigue starts to build. Exercising those muscles first also helps you continue to warm up.
- Target one muscle group, then its opposite. For example, pair quadriceps and hamstring workouts, or biceps curls with triceps dips. This maintains symmetry and balance and allows each muscle group to recover while you are working its opposite.
- Use variations carefully. In any one workout, it is usually better to perform distinctly different exercises than to do variations of the same exercise. For example, doing three different kinds of push-ups affords variety and increases the intensity of the workout, but it is more effective to do one type of push-up and then, say, a bench press.
- Work steadily and slowly. Quick, explosive movements make you work hard at the beginning of a repetition, but

continued

that initial burst can carry the muscle through the rest of the movement. A slow, controlled movement subjects the muscle to relatively consistent stress during both the lifting and lowering phase of the exercise.

- Breathe continuously. Holding your breath can spike your blood pressure. Generally, you should exhale during the straining part of the exercise, such as when you move weights away from your body, and inhale during the easier part, such as when you move them toward your body.

- Use a full range of motion. For each repetition, move the joint through its maximum extension and flexion. A muscle that makes only a partial movement does less work and can lose flexibility. On the other hand, don't flex or extend so far that the joint is suddenly bearing the load—that's the muscle's job.

- Rest intelligently between sets. If your rest interval is too short, you will exhaust the muscle group; if too long, the next set won't make you work harder, which it should. One to two minutes is usually sufficient between sets.

- Cool down. Abruptly ending a workout can cause blood to pool in the extremities, creating a sudden drop in blood pressure that may produce light-headedness or fainting. Finish with a run in place or repeat your warmup.

- Keep track of your progress. Record reps, sets, and weights for each exercise every week. Some muscles will respond more quickly than others, so you will need to increase the overload at different rates.

Stretching. In addition to making you feel good, stretching promotes flexibility. Being flexible is an integral part of overall fitness, and it's especially critical for cavers, who are forever twisting and turning, reaching and writhing.

Good flexibility reduces the chance of injury. Muscles that restrict the natural range of motion in the joints are more susceptible to pulls, tears, and stress injuries than those that are flexible enough to allow a full range of motion. Tight calf muscles, for example, can place undue stress on the foot, leading to orthopedic problems, including painful Achilles tendinitis. A joint is flexible when the muscles and connective tissues around it do not restrict its natural range of motion.

Stretching a muscle requires an external force supplied by gravity, by the contraction of an opposing muscle, or by a stretching partner. To increase a muscle's length, studies show, you must regularly pull it about 10 percent beyond its normal length. That's the point at which your muscle feels stretched enough to be slightly uncomfortable but not enough to cause pain. You should progress to where you can hold the position for twenty to thirty seconds, relax, and then repeat the stretch three to five times.

The approach in a progressive stretching program is similar to the overload principle used to build muscle strength. To increase flexibility, you must regularly stretch the muscle slightly beyond its normal length. It will adapt to this overload and reward you with a greater range of joint motion.

The muscles most in need of stretching are the ones on which you place the greatest demands. Reasonably active people should routinely stretch the calves (to increase the range of motion in ankles and to prevent calf pain and Achilles tendinitis), hamstrings, gluteals, and lower back (to prevent epidemic lower-back problems), inner thighs (to reduce the chance of groin pulls), quadriceps and hip flexors (to prevent knee stiffness), and upper back, chest, and shoulders (to prevent rounded shoulders and restricted range of motion).

There are three basic types of stretching: ballistic, static, and contract-relax. Avoid ballistic stretching in which you stretch to your limit and perform quick, repetitive bouncing movements. This produces the "stretch reflex," a nearly instantaneous contraction, which raises the risk of soft-tissue injury.

You can override this stretch reflex by doing a sustained or static stretch, which is slow and gentle, never sudden or drastic. A static stretch is a gradual stretch through a muscle's full range of movement until you feel resistance. Pushing into that resistance, but backing off from pain, hold the maximum position for three to thirty seconds (depending on how far you have progressed), relax, and then repeat several times. You can increase a static stretch by using an external force, such as someone gently pushing against your raised leg.

The longest stretch of all is possible with the contract-relax method. This technique has three parts. First, do a conventional static stretch. As you begin to feel the stretch, reverse the motion and push against your partner as hard as you can (the contract phase), using only the muscles you are trying to stretch. After five or six seconds, relax and let your partner ease the muscles back into a stretch that extends them farther than before. Together, you should hold this

Here are some stretching tips:
- Choose a time of day when you are unlikely to be interrupted. Stretching requires concentration and patience. Don't rush through your routines.
- Wear loose-fitting clothing that doesn't restrict your movement. For comfort's sake, do not wear a belt or jewelry.
- Stretching should always be preceded by a five- to ten-minute warmup, such as slow jogging or riding a stationary bicycle. This increases blood flow and raises muscle temperature, both vital for muscle elasticity. Stretching while muscles are cold may strain or tear them.
- Don't force a stretch. If there's any pain, back off. At worst, any discomfort should be mild and brief. Remember that your flexibility changes from day to day and that you may not be able to perform the same stretch on one day that you did the day before.
- An optimal stretching session should last ten to twenty minutes, with each stretch held at least three seconds. Gradually work up to holding for twenty to thirty seconds.

continued

- Begin by stretching major muscle groups, then stretch the specific muscles required for your sport or activity. Pay attention to the body parts that are the least flexible and stretch them more often.
- Breathe evenly. Breathing rapidly or irregularly or holding your breath may make you tense. Instead, go into a stretch as you are exhaling, and then concentrate on breathing normally and slowly.
- Stretch within an hour before starting your activity.
- Don't bounce. Stretching should be gradual and relaxed.
- Try to isolate the muscles you want to stretch. If other parts of the body move, there will be less benefit to the target muscle.
- Work for bilateral flexibility—that is, equal flexibility on both sides of your body. When stretching one side of the body, be sure to follow with the same stretches on the other side.
- Stretch *after* vigorous exercise as well as before. This prevents muscles from tightening up quickly and lessens the chance of soreness.
- Don't give up because you are less flexible than others. And never try to compete with another person by seeing who is more flexible. Flexibility varies from person to person. What's important is your own improvement. It may take months, but if you stay with it, you will become more flexible.
- Stretch three to seven days a week to increase flexibility. To maintain flexibility, three days a week is probably adequate.
- Keep track of your progress. Test your general flexibility at the beginning of your training program to establish your flexibility baseline. Then retest your suppleness monthly as you progress.

position for twenty to thirty seconds. This method not only produces the greatest flexibility, but also increases strength.

Watch Your Weight. Stay (or become) slim. Because of the great variety of activities involved in caving, it is impossible to describe the ideal caver's body, as is often done in other sports. What is certain, however, is that being overweight is disadvantageous. Not only is it difficult to move a wider body through squeezes, it also means more weight for the legs to carry and the arms to lift.

Libraries and bookstores are well stocked with diet books. But beware—many of them tout bogus theories, such as the weight-loss benefits of a high-protein diet. And others tell you what you already know: "If you consume a thousand calories a day, you will eventually lose weight."

Recent research suggests that it's not just the number of calories you consume and burn that causes weight gain or loss, but also which types of food those calories come from. A study from Harvard Medical School found that after adjusting for age, physical activity, alcohol, and smoking, there was only a limited correlation between caloric intake and body weight. Excess weight was more strongly linked to fat consumption, especially saturated fat. In other words, the proportion of daily calories that comes from fat, not simply the number of calories, correlates highly with total body weight and percentage of body fat.

GETTING UNSTUCK

Almost anyone who has been caving for very long has gotten stuck, at least briefly. Floyd Collins notwithstanding, the problem is usually solved quickly by following these steps:

- Be certain you are really stuck. Often retreating slightly to remove your pack, helmet, or overalls is enough to make the difference. Sometimes another caver can unhook the obstruction and free you.
- Relax. This makes you more pliable, and you may simply slide free.
- If you are sure you can no longer help yourself, the other members of your party may be able to grab you and pull you free.

YOUR BODY MASS INDEX

How to determine a person's "desirable" weight is still a matter of controversy, but most experts agree that the preferred way is to measure the proportion of fat in your body. You can estimate this by calculating your body mass index—the figure you get by dividing your weight in kilograms by the square of your height in meters. This is a useful figure for cavers, because it minimizes the effect of height and provides reasonable guidelines for defining overweight.

Calculate your body mass index by following the steps below. Weigh yourself in shorts or underwear. Round off numbers after the decimal point to the nearest hundredth.

1. To convert your weight to kilograms, divide the pounds by 2.2 (the number of pounds per kilogram): _____. (For example, I weigh 180 pounds. Divide 180 by 2.2 to get 81.82 kilograms.)

2. To convert your height to meters, divide height in inches (without shoes) by 39.4 (the number of inches in one meter): _____. (I'm 73 inches. Divide 73 by 39.4 to get 1.85 meters.) Take this figure and square it: _____. ($1.85 \times 1.85 = 3.42$)

3. Divide the result of (1) by (2): _____. ($81.82 \div 3.42 = 24$) This is your body mass figure.

For men, desirable body mass ranges from 20 to 25. Above about 29 is obese; above 40 is extremely obese.

For women, desirable body mass is 19 to 24; obesity begins at about 27, and extreme obesity is above 39.

For both men and women, values below 19 are underweight.

- The members of your party can tie a figure-eight loop in a rope or sling and thread it through the passageway for you to use as a handhold, enabling them to pull you out.

In crawlways known to be tight, send the smallest caver through first, carrying a line that can then be used as a hand-hold or foothold by the following cavers.

Never descend headfirst into a steep, unknown crawlway. It's too hard to retreat by backing uphill. Also, the passage may flare out, leaving you with no more support than Alice had when she tumbled into the rabbit hole.

- You or another caver can place the loop around one of your feet. Push off hard with your foot until you slide forward at least a few inches. Raise your knee, have the others take up the slack, and push off again. This should extricate you from the tightest squeezes.
- If all of these attempts fail, which is extremely rare, the other members of your party should supply you with food and fluids and keep you warm and reassured, while someone goes for help.

6

Advanced Techniques

Technique will take a vertical caver much farther than brute strength and determination, although it's nice to have all three. Substituting physical power for technique results in sloppy climbing and quickly depletes energy. The result may be retreat or failure.

Technique means using your body and equipment efficiently and properly. If you can accomplish this, you will likely be a safe and successful vertical caver. So take your time and learn how to do each procedure correctly the first time, because bad habits are hard to break.

This chapter by itself will not enable you to master the techniques of vertical caving, but it will provide necessary background, a head start if you will, allowing you to progress more quickly when you get out in the field with an instructor.

VERTICAL RIGGING

Rigging, or the correct anchoring of a fixed rope to provide a safe descent and ascent, is the first link in the chain of your vertical caving system. Just because you've rigged ropes for rock climbing, rescue, or window washing doesn't mean you know how to do it properly for caving. The concept is different.

The goal of the surface free climber is not to use the rope to pull himself up or let himself down, but to have it there as an emergency backup, like a tightrope walker's safety net. A rock climber sets multiple anchors so that if one fails during a fall, others will stop him.

And climbers prefer a dynamic rope, which will stretch during a fall, absorbing much of the energy. The entire system of dynamic rope, anchors, and belays is geared to protect a falling climber.

By contrast, when rigging a rope for vertical caving, the goal is to construct a nylon highway. The anchored rope, your only means of entering and leaving the cave, is supposed to be climbed upon but not come loose. You usually cannot rig another rope should an anchor fail. If it does fail, someone will probably be injured, and those below the faulty anchor may be stranded.

In vertical caving, keep the rigging simple and strong. The ideal is a static rope tied around a natural anchor, with at least one backup anchor and no slack in between the primary anchor and the secondary ones.

When your life depends on a single rope, it simply cannot be allowed to fail. This means it must be rigged so that there is no chance that the knots will come loose or the rope will be cut. If a pit is right at the cave entrance, look for a sturdy tree to provide a bombproof natural rig point. Sometimes stable boulders or rock outcrops can be used. When you lack a bombproof natural anchor, you may be able to direct the naturally anchored rope through an artificial anchor placed out on the wall to create a secure free drop. Try to use environmentally friendly chocks and Friends before turning to pitons and bolts.

Clear away all loose rock, debris, and foliage from near the top of the drop before the rope is lowered over the side. Set such debris back away from the lip so that it can't topple into the pit. As the lead caver descends, she should be on the lookout for further loose rock that might be dislodged by the rope or other cavers. If possible, she should clean it out so that it can't do any damage, taking care not to drop rocks on people or on the rope coiled below.

Another way of avoiding rope-rock contact on long drops is to rebelay, setting an anchor below the point of potential abrasion. Even though you are using one continuous rope, you rig it as if it were two drops. In this way, the abrasive rock is at the bottom of the first section of rope. And because the rope is continuous, the anchor is naturally backed up. Alternatively, attach a sling to an anchor to pull the rope away from a rub point.

You may have to estimate the length of the drop in order to choose the correct length of rope. If you can't look over the edge and see the bottom, drop a rock (after ensuring that nobody is below) and note the time it takes for the rock to reach the bottom. Plug that number into one of the following formulas:

- To determine the depth in meters: $D = 5t^2$ (squared), where D is the depth in meters and t is the time in seconds.
- To determine the depth in feet: $D = 89.7(t) - 156$.

Keep in mind that this drop is not taking place in a vacuum and that results will be slightly affected by atmospheric factors, such as humidity, altitude, and temperature, and by shape and density of the rock itself. And the longer the drop, the longer it takes for the sound to reach you. Another potential problem is that the rock may not make an unhindered free fall. If it hits a ledge, you may misinterpret it as the bottom of the pit. Alternatively, your rock may hit a ledge and dislodge a second rock, which continues to the bottom; such a delay could lead you to estimate the drop to be deeper than it really is.

When rigging a wet pitch, inspect it very carefully for rub points that might be obscured by flowing water. Do not leave a rope rigged in moving water unless absolutely necessary. The abrasion resistance of nylon rope is reduced when wet. Often the last caver down can pull the rope to the side, out of the water's path, and tie it off until it is needed for the trip out.

Inside a cave, look for natural anchors, such as boulders, flakes, ribs, and speleothems, taking care not to deface formations. Some argue that speleothems should not be used at all, but slinging a column is generally much less destructive than the alternative—setting artificial protection.

Always inspect the formation to which you intend to anchor the rope. Make sure it is attached to solid rock and not to an insecure base of dirt, mud, or clay. Look for burrs, ridges, and spikes, the tiniest irregularities sharp enough to abrade the rope. If they will be in contact with your rope, pad them.

Because of their orderly crystalline structure, speleothems tend to cleave. Reject any speleothem with a diameter smaller than about $2^3/4$ inches. To reduce leverage, rig the anchor close to where the formation attaches to the floor, wall, or ceiling.

With many speleothems, you can use tensionless rigging. Wrap the rope several times around the formation, and tie a figure-eight loop or bowline through which the fixed rope passes. It's often preferable to wrap a 1-inch tubular webbing sling around the feature and then clip the rope into the webbing. The webbing, flatter with more surface area, tends to hold the rock better.

The bowline knot is used to create a loop at the end of the rope for attaching to, say, a tree or carabiner. Although the bowline is still used by cavers, many have switched to the figure-eight knot. The latter has many of the same applications, but it is easier to inspect and doesn't need to be backed up with an overhand knot to prevent accidental untying. The water knot (double overhand) is generally used to tie ends of flat webbing together. The double fisherman's knot, or grapevine, is used to join two ropes. It is effective even if the two ropes are of different diameters.

The person rigging the drop should be familiar with the range of rigging options. He should know the stress limits of his equipment and how to avoid excess stress. Even if someone else in your party is an "expert" and does the rigging, it's important that you and every vertical caver in your party learn the art and science of rigging. You may be forced to take over in an emergency. Besides, every member of the party should check and recheck the rigging for errors. After all, they have a big stake in it, too.

PRUSIKING

Ascending was originally done with knots and no mechanical ascenders. The original technique, called *prusiking,* was developed in

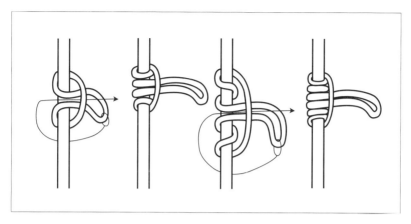

The prusik knot

Austria by Karl Prusik and described in the *Austrian Alpine Journal* in 1931. The knot he devised still bears his name, as does the general technique of ascending rope with knots or mechanical ascenders.

Although other knots have come and gone, the prusik knot is still the knot of choice of those who use knots in lieu of mechanical ascenders. Even if you have a vertical pack full of ascenders, you should be able to prusik in case of equipment shortage or failure.

Climbing with knots has its advantages, especially for a beginner. A cheap, compact, lightweight way to get started in vertical caving, it allows you to improve your rope-climbing skills in a low-tech way. The system requires you to become proficient in tying a variety of knots besides the prusik, including the figure-eight, bowline, double fisherman's, and helical—but any caver who intends to do single rope technique (SRT) should have a firm command of these knots anyway. Caver Robert Zimmerman says that he has had no trouble teaching beginners from seven to fifty years old to climb 80-foot cliffs with knots.

For prusiking, you will need the following equipment:
- Seat harness
- 15 feet of 2-inch flat webbing
- 1 aluminum D-shape screw-link carabiner

- 1 aluminum locking D carabiner
- 1 figure-eight
- 40 feet of flexible 7-millimeter prusik cord sold in climbing shops

Building a Knot System

If you plan to use knots as your primary system, both a seat and chest harness are desirable. A seat harness takes pressure off the chest and provides a rest position for long ascents. But using only a seat harness puts the balance point a little low, so it's better to route slings through a chest harness.

Wearing your caving boots, take one end of the prusik cord and fashion a foot loop with either a figure-eight knot or a double fisherman's knot. With the knot above the foot, slip the loop over the boot, twist it underneath, bring it over the top, twist again, and then bring it under the boot and wrap it around the ankle.

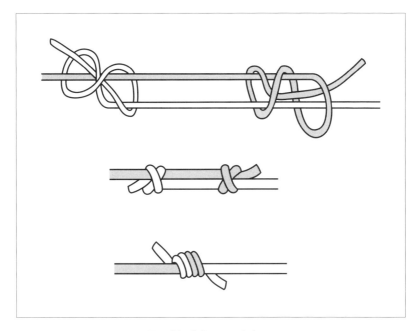

Double fisherman's knot

Adjust the size of the loop so that the knot is no more than 3 inches above the top of your foot. Leave about $2^1/2$ inches of cord above the knot. After this first loop is fitted to your foot, lift the cord to your knee and let the rest of the cord drop to the ground. Add 3 or 4 inches, cut the cord at that point, and burn both ends. Use the new end to make the second leg loop. Once it is adjusted properly on your foot, lift the cord to your crotch and let the rest of the cord drop. Cut it here and burn both ends.

Take the remaining piece of cord and tie a small figure-eight on a bight near the end. The loop only has to be big enough to fit onto a screw-link. After slipping the figure-eight knot onto the carabiner attached to your seat harness, lift the cord to your chin, add a little extra, and cut it there.

The cord that's left is used to make a prusik loop, using a double fisherman's knot. Adjust the length so that when it is attached to your seat harness with a locking carabiner, it will also attach to the rope above the helical knot described below.

Using the Knot System

Using helical knots, tie the bottom foot loop to the main rope just above the knee, and tie the other foot loop to the main rope just below the crotch. Tie the upper cord to the main rope no higher than your neck.

As you climb, stay seated in your harness as much as possible. Keep your legs tucked under your buttocks and your head forward. This keeps you vertical and stops you from flipping backward. From this seated position, you will lift your legs to create slack in the cords, and then slide the foot knots upward. In one motion, stand and slide the top knot up, then immediately sit down again.

In order to become more efficient, practice simultaneously standing and sliding the top knot, and then sitting as soon as the knot has been raised to its maximum. In time you should be able to keep your body upright. If not, add a simple chest harness, either a commercial version or one made out of 8 feet of 1-inch tubular webbing, a ladder buckle, and a carabiner. Thread the upper ascender through the carabiner to keep the climber close to the rope and upright.

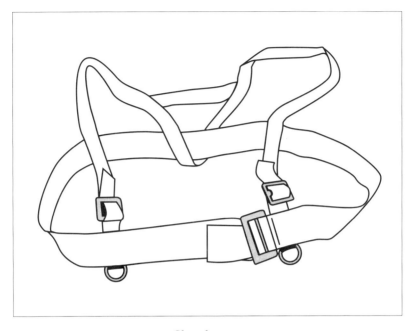

Chest harness

Inspect the prusik cord often for wear and tear. The upper knot will wear most quickly and should be replaced when it begins to fray, usually after a dozen or so trips.

ROPE CARE AND MANAGEMENT

Because the rope is such an important piece of caving gear, it's imperative that you take care of it. Besides keeping it clean, you have to avoid kinks and knots by careful coiling or by using a rope bag. Rope management is especially critical for the belayer, who must feed out the rope smoothly to the leader.

One method is called *pooling,* laying one end of the rope on the ground, then piling it carefully in concentric loops. In this way, the top of the pile should feed out smoothly without kinks or knots. Avoid dirt by putting your backpack on the ground and then piling your rope on top of it. Be sure to keep track of both ends of the rope.

Temple of the Cave Fire-God, Three Fingers, New Mexico

Unusual lava tube with a lake, Hawaii

*Caver ignites under-
water flashes from
raft, Grand Canyon*

Cave crab, Belize

Caver following a whitewater river, Grand Canyon

Large stalactite clusters, Virgin Cave, New Mexico

*Caver rappelling by a waterfall,
Sistema Chichicasapan, Mexico*

*Cavers on rope in a 400-foot
pit, Sotano del Soconusco*

Sunbeam shines into a 90-foot pit, Cova Negre, Spain

Falls below cave entrance, El Chorreadero, Mexico

Caver peering over rimstone dams, Crystal Sequoia, California

Caver at the entrance to Tower Place, Lechuguilla, New Mexico

Cluster of formations by the
Pearlsian Gulf, Lechuguilla,
New Mexico

Caver beneath large
flowstone, Ogle
Cave, New Mexico

Caver climbing the falls, El Chorreadero, Mexico

Lava river cave, Oregon

Another method is known as *lap coiling,* in which you feed the rope through a loop of webbing—a runner—to help keep it organized.

Probably your best option is a *rope bag.* Stuff your rope in the bag, carry it to the cave, and enjoy a clean feed once you're there.

Don't confuse rope management with an obsession with neatness; it can be a matter of life or death. Belayers with rope problems must be able to solve them without pulling the lead off the rock.

After the climb, you must recoil your ropes. Sit down and loop the rope around a knee and a foot, making big coils. Repeatedly wrap the last 5 or 6 feet of rope around the loops to keep them in place. You can also make a mountaineer's coil, in which you form loops and use leftover rope to make shoulder straps and a waist belt. You can wear it like a backpack—if you don't already have a backpack.

BELAYING

The two principal belaying activities are paying out rope to the climber and stopping the rope from paying out if he falls. As a general rule, cavers should belay more often than they do. Belaying is one of the few times in life when you literally have someone else's life in your hands. Most cavers, realizing its deadly importance, become conscientious belayers.

Once upon a time, before belay devices, there was the body belay. In this antiquated technique, the belayer wraps the rope around his back just above the hips. The "live" end of the rope, the end going to the climber, is gripped in the left hand (guide hand). The right hand (brake hand) holds the rope on the other side of the body. The idea is that the friction caused by the rope traveling around the belayer's body will allow the belayer to gain control of the rope in case the climber falls.

The body belay is the riskiest way to belay. Friction is created by the belayer's precious body, so there's a risk of rope burns on the back and hands. Today most cavers and climbers create friction with a belay device, such as a figure-eight or a Sticht plate, allowing them to lock the rope tight in case of a fall.

The same rules apply with a belay device as with a body belay. In either case, the belay is controlled by a guide hand and a brake hand, and the brake hand never leaves the rope. Belayers must be alert, ready to react at the first sign of trouble.

It's critical that the lines of communication remain open between belay and climber. If there are any problems, the belayer should notify the climber immediately, and vice versa. Of course, it helps if the two are speaking the same language. About a dozen basic signals enable climbers to say what needs to be said:

"On belay?" says the caver before starting.

"Belay on," replies the belayer when ready.

"Climbing," says the caver before starting.

"Climb," responds the belayer when ready to belay.

"Up rope," says the caver wanting the slack pulled in.

"Slack," says the caver wanting the belayer to let out rope.

"Tension," says the caver wanting the belayer to hold him tight.

"Rock!" shouts the caver when loose rock is falling.

"Watch me!" says the caver feeling especially vulnerable.

"Falling!" says the caver feeling even more vulnerable.

"Belay off," says the caver after feeling safe and secure.

"Off belay," replies the belayer to indicate the belay has ended.

"Rope," says the caver to indicate a rope is being dropped.

ANCHORING

Natural Anchors

Natural anchors are objects to which you might anchor that were not put in the rock by humans. For example, you might girth-hitch to a sturdy tree or tie on to a knob of rock, always ensuring that it will take a downward pull.

You can also loop webbing over a horn or flake, but be sure it's not a detached flake. Test by tugging. On many occasions you will find little rock tunnels through which you can string webbing and attach protection. Also common are natural chockstones, boulders wedged in cracks.

Artificial Placements

Putting artificial anchors in the rock may be necessary when natural anchors are unavailable. In most cases, you will make the placement, attach a carabiner and a sling, and then clip the rope into the sling.

Nuts. When placing chocks, hexentrics, and stoppers, search the rock for gaps, and search the gaps for tiny irregularities. Since a nut has to be able to hold a downward pull, you want the down side of the crack to bottleneck, to be smaller than the nut. Wedged in that part of the crack, it should not pull out. The beauty of this type of placement is that it will hold a fall while doing no damage to the rock.

Hexentrics, depending on how they're turned, offer several different configurations. That means a single hex can work in different-size cracks.

Stoppers and hexentrics are great in expanding cracks because you do no hammering. They're also perfect for the bottom of piton scars. Repeated piton use opens up the top of a crack, but down at the bottom, where it narrows, it's receptive to hexes and stoppers.

Spring-Loaded Camming Devices. Ideally, SLCDs should be placed so that all the cams are touching the rock surface inside the crack. You can place them so that only two cams are touching rock, and they will probably hold your body weight until you can put in better protection; however, don't count on those two cams to hold a fall.

Align the stem in the direction of pull. Try not to offset the cams, as that diminishes the holding power. Avoid a tipped placement, with the cams wide open. Ideally, the cams should be positioned at midrange.

Avoid rocking the cam tips. Clip your rope to a sling long enough to ensure that you won't move the SLCD as you climb past it. Don't cram an oversize SLCD into an undersize placement; it may make removal difficult or impossible.

One advantage of a camming device is that the more weight you put on it, the more it expands and grips the crack. If cams pull out, it's almost certainly because you haven't set them properly. For example, if the inside of the crack is composed of loose flakes, you may accidentally wedge the SLCD against flakes instead of solid rock. Test the placement by attaching a piece of webbing and giving a tug. If you pay attention to detail, you needn't worry about camming devices pulling out. Anytime you need an anchor and can use an SLCD, do so.

Because they are complex, Friends occasionally jam or malfunction. They also have a tendency to work their way farther into a crack. Here are some suggestions for minimizing problems:

- Do not place the Friend too deep in the crack. When it's time to extract it, the cam-release trigger may be out of reach.
- Realign the Friend if one or more of the cams do not bite into the crack walls.
- Don't let the cams invert, thereby losing their holding power.
- Avoid placements where the cams are too wide. Try a larger Friend.
- For the best performance, the size of the Friend should be such that the cam-release trigger is in the middle third of its total length of travel in the retaining slot.
- Always close the cams completely and allow them to expand inside the crack.
- Minimize movement by the Friend by making sure it is connected properly to the rest of the climbing system.
- Keep Friends off the ground and away from dirt particles.
- If the movement becomes stiff, spray the moving parts with a lubricant like WD40; do not use oil.
- If you have trouble with extraction, carry a special retrieving tool.

Pitons. If you can't find a spot for a nut or a cam, you may have to pound in a piton. They come in a wide range of sizes to fit cracks both thick and thin. Pitons share a common trait: When hammered in properly, all (except the tiny rurp) make a high-pitched ringing sound, almost bell-like. If you hear more of a dull thud, chances are the placement is insecure. Regardless of pitch, give the placement a tug, then a bounce; if it seems secure, check whether it will hold your body weight before counting on it to hold a fall.

If a piton won't go in a crack very far, you can tie a short piece of nylon webbing, called a *tie-off loop* or a *hero loop,* to the piton near the rock. Known as "tying off short," this technique reduces leverage, effectively placing less weight on the questionable piton.

Bolts. If you can't find cracks or natural protection, you may have to drill a hole in the rock. Do this manually with a masonry drill bit, either a star drive or a rawl drive—no power drills should be used. The standard hole, $1/4$ inch in diameter and $11/2$ inches deep, is created by tapping the drill bit against the rock and twisting. It's not uncommon to take twenty to thirty minutes to achieve this, depending on the sharpness of the drill bits and the hardness of the rock. When you're finished, the bolt stud you hammer into the hole should be slightly larger than the hole itself to ensure snugness. Attached to the bolt is a bolt hanger, a strip of metal with two holes. The smaller hole accommodates the bolt; the larger, a carabiner.

Bolts are permanent—and therefore controversial. They usually are placed only at the top when there are no other options available. Carry a bolt kit whenever exploring a new vertical cave.

Where to Anchor

Deciding where to place an anchor is a tug-of-war between the available and the possible. Questions abound. How big is the crack? Will it accept your first choice, a camming device? How about a stopper, your second choice. Or is it more hole than crack, suitable only for a larger piton?

When lead climbing, it's important to remember that you don't have to place the next piece of protection far away. You might put in the next piece only a couple of feet from the previous piece, especially if it's the most secure place available. You may only gain a couple of feet, but so what? At least it's progress.

CLEANING PROTECTION
Chocks

Removing, or cleaning, chocks can be a challenge, especially if they've held a fall. Even without a fall, a chock has withstood the downward pull of your equipment and body weight. Just weighting that nut, which is probably softer than the rock, will have set it quite well.

To remove a chock, first try lifting it out in the opposite direction from which it went in. Climb above the chock and yank in an upward direction. Still stuck? Wiggle it, or tap it with a carabiner.

(Don't use a hammer on a chock unless absolutely necessary, because it will deform the chock, possibly ruining it.) If that doesn't work, take out your nut tool, a thin, 9-inch piece of metal that looks like an old ruler with notches in it, giving you more possibilities when you're trying to pry out the nut.

If you are still stymied, you can place a Lost Arrow piton against the nut and tap it with a hammer in an upward direction. Remember to tie on everything you're working with. If you have a Lost Arrow in one hand and a hammer in the other, you will lose an unconnected chock when it pops out.

Spring-Loaded Camming Devices

SLCDs are usually easy to remove. Squeezing the trigger reduces the profile, which should permit easy extraction. Sometimes, though, a cam can be stubborn, especially if it's been extended to the maximum. Once in a while, it will move within a crack after you've climbed past it. Rope drag is the culprit, causing the cam to wiggle up and down (called *walking*) and making it hard even to reach it. If that's your problem, you may need a tool called a Friend of a Friend. This extender fits onto the stem of a Friend, allowing you to reach farther into the crack than you could with your fingers.

Pitons

Pitons can be the toughest cleaning problems. The first step is to try to loosen the piton by hammering it up and down. Hammer it down as far as you can, then turn the hammer and pound it back up to its limit. Do that back and forth a few times until you feel it loosen.

If it remains defiant, use a "cleaner biner": Clip a junk carabiner to the piton, attach a piece of webbing to it, and attach the webbing to your harness. As you hammer the piton up and down, your weight pulls on it, making removal more likely. And when it finally pops, you won't lose it.

Alternatively, you can put the pick end of your hammer through the eye of the piton and use the added leverage to pry it out over your shoulder. To prevent the piton from flying off behind you, keep one hand on the hammer and the other on the piton.

USING RUNNERS

Runners are loops of tubular nylon webbing about 6 feet long that are used to sling a rock or a speleothem or to prevent rope drag on climbs that veer or zigzag up and down a rock. When rope doesn't run in a straight line, a caver is fighting not only gravity and the weight of the equipment, but also resistance from the rope, which seems to want to pull him off the rock. Well-placed runners will reguide the rope so that it runs in a fairly straight line.

Sometimes you can't fix the problem with runners. If you're zigging and zagging all over the rock and can't completely overcome rope drag, then at least be more patient. There's no point in yelling at your partner, who is feeding the rope as smoothly as possible.

RAPPELLING

Rappelling can refer to either the climber's practice of descending a doubled rope and pulling it down afterward or the caver's practice of descending on a single rope. If Hollywood movies are to be believed, speed rappelling is a sport in its own right. Actually, rappelling is a *controlled* means of sliding down a rope, one often used by cavers to enter a cave.

Historically called *roping down*, the favored technique until recently was the Dulfursitz, or body, rappel. It's the only method that uses no mechanical devices on the rope. Friction to slow the descent is created by the rope rubbing against the rappeller's body. The obvious potential for pain during a body rappel was no doubt an incentive to create mechanical descenders. Today the body rappel is as obsolete as the icebox. It is strictly a survival skill, used only when no other gadgets are available. Still, you should learn how to perform a body rappel in case of emergency. First, face the anchors and straddle the rock. Then bring the rope around behind you, across one hip, up across the chest like a bandolier, over the shoulder, and down the back.

After the body rappel came the carabiner brake, a configuration of six carabiners attached to the climbing harness and positioned so that when a rope is threaded through them, enough friction is created to slow a descent.

Basic rappel

The carabiner brake will still work, but it has been replaced by simpler gadgets, such as the figure-eight and the caver's favorite, the rappel rack, both of which work on the same principle that if you bend a rope with enough angle, you will create enough friction to slow descent.

Even though rappel devices have made the job safer and easier, you should still be vigilant before and during a rappel. It is arguably the most dangerous part of the caving expedition. Make sure hair and clothing are well clear of the friction device and incapable of becoming entangled.

The scariest part of the rappel is usually the start, especially if you have to go over a lip. Once the rope is weighted, keep your feet planted about shoulder width, and let out some rope until you are leaning well back. Begin the rappel by backpedaling. Stability is increased when you keep the legs spread about shoulder width and nearly perpendicular to the wall. If you drop your feet too far, they will skid off, slamming you against the wall. Twist your upper torso toward your brake hand, and you will be able to look down.

LADDER CLIMBING

Cable ladders, a traditional favorite of cavers, are still used for short drops. In a compact package about 12 by 9 by 6 inches, you get 33 feet of pit-climbing capability. For short drops, it's much cheaper, lighter, faster, and easier than having everyone in your group use his own ascenders.

Here are some rappel tips:
- When learning to rappel, top ropes are safest.
- Stay tied into the belay when sorting out ropes.
- Make sure anchors are safe.
- Make sure your partners are ready before you drop ropes down to them.
- Tie knots in the ends of your rope to ensure that you won't slide off the end.
- Lower rope ends gently to avoid dislodging rocks or tangling ropes.
- Make sure the ropes reach the bottom of the drop.
- Rappel as smoothly as possible to avoid cutting the rope or dislodging rocks. Don't go too fast—no more than about 40 feet per minute, and slower is better.
- Give a clear signal only when untied from the rope and out of the rockfall zone.
- Make sure knots have been untied for retrieval.

Your first step is a psychological one—convincing yourself that anything that looks so fragile will actually support your weight. That done, practice with your ladder on the surface, perhaps rigging it to hang free from a tree limb. Climbing a cable ladder is strenuous, but proper technique will make the job much easier. Rely on the stronger leg muscles for most of the work. Use the arms primarily for balance.

Begin by facing the ladder and placing one foot (let's say it's the left) behind the ladder on the bottom rung. Then bring the left hand around behind the ladder and grasp a rung at a comfortable height above your head, fingers pointed toward your body. With that grip secure, shift your weight up onto the first rung and place the right foot on the second rung, this time on the front of the ladder. The right hand is now placed above the left hand, either on the front or back, whichever is more comfortable.

Caver climbing a ladder

By alternating the placement of your feet, front and back on every other rung, you prevent the ladder from flying away from you. This works well if the ladder is hanging free, but not so well when the ladder is pressed tightly against rock. The solution then is to maneuver the ladder away from the wall so that your hands and feet can get at the rungs. One way to do this is to force the ladder sideways, a method that takes a bit of strength but is easy to maintain once accomplished. Another way is to place both feet on the front side, bend at the waist and knees, and push the ladder away from the rock with the toes of your boots.

Belay every ladder climb, no matter how short. It's rare that a ladder will break, but it is possible to fall off if you're tired or it's slippery. To set up a belay, use a rope long enough that you can double it through a carabiner at the top, and then bottom-belay the first one up and the last one down. Tie into the belay line with a bowline on a coil.

The last ladder climber can use a short length of rope to attach the bottom of the ladder to her seat harness or some other tie-off point. In this way, the ladder follows the climber as she climbs, making it easier to unsnag it from projections.

When rigging a ladder, select an anchor point two or three rungs above the lip. This makes it far less strenuous to negotiate the last few feet.

When lowering a ladder, always ask if the drop is clear and yell, "Rope!" before lowering it. Watch where it goes, if you can do so safely. Pay out the ladder slowly, trying to avoid snag points and niches too narrow for your body. The first person rappelling down should check the ladder's routing to make sure it's safe and secure.

When lowering the belay rope for the next climber, be sure it doesn't pass through the ladder, which can lead to a nasty surprise.

FREE-CLIMBING TECHNIQUES
Hand Techniques

The emphasis here is on using features as handholds—that is, holding on to knobs, protrusions, pockets, edges, or slopes. In general, there are two ways to grab edges with the fingers: *crimping* and *open-hand techniques.*

Crimping. This involves grabbing a hold so that the fingers are in a scrunched-up position. Usually it's necessary to crimp the worst holds, like small "dime edges" and incut flakes. Crimping requires more strength, stresses the tendons of the hands more, and puts them at greater risk for injury than open-hand techniques.

Open-Hand Techniques. If you face a little larger, or positive, edge, open-hand the hold, as it lets more of the skeletal system of the hand bear the brunt. Grab on like it's a chin-up bar or the rung of a ladder, with an open, relaxed hand.

Whether you are forced to crimp or able to use an open-hand technique, always remember to conserve energy and never pull harder than you have to.

Palming is an open-hand technique in which you put the entire palm, or maybe the last three knuckles, straight in on the rock. It is used on bigger holds and slopes. It relies on the friction between the rock and the skin of the palm and is usually used with an inward and downward push. It can be a tenuous hold, because if you move the hand slightly and break the friction, you may start sliding. This is because dynamic friction is less than static friction. That is, once something is moving, it takes less force to keep it moving than it did to break it from its static position. The trick is to prevent such movement in the first place.

Remember, these hand techniques are not always used with a downward pull. At times it is necessary to use side pulls (inward to outward force, or vice versa) or even upward pulls, depending on body positioning and the move being attempted.

Chimneys

Squeeze Chimneys. It's rare to have a crack so thin that you can't get your chest in it but wide enough to accept an elbow for an elbow lock. Usually, if the elbow will fit the chest will fit too, as in a narrow, or squeeze, chimney.

You can climb squeeze chimneys using off-width techniques with a few added variations, one of which is a knee bar. Assuming you have a secure hold with your upper body, put your knees flush against the chest side of the crack, kind of a baby's kneeling position with the feet splayed out and the heels pressed against the other side of the crack. With both legs doing this, you can support your body weight. To move is difficult, however, because you don't have a lot of flexibility in this position.

The climbing sequence in a squeeze chimney goes like this: While supporting your upper body with one palm pressing downward against a wall and the other limb in an elbow lock, wiggle one hip and one knee up, set it, shift to the other side, and wiggle it up in an S-like movement. It's a worm simulation, the vertical equivalent of army maneuvers in which soldiers crawl under fences in a side-to-side squiggle.

Classic Chimneys. When cracks are so wide that they may be easily entered, you can no longer use an elbow lock or a knee bar wedge. Now you are in a classic chimney. In this size crack, you lose a certain amount of security but gain ease of climbing.

The technique for classic chimneys is as follows: One foot is against the side of the crack you are facing; the other foot is tucked under your buttocks against the other side. Your hands are pressed against the back wall, stabilizing you, but most of the work is done by the lower body. Move the upper body up as high as you can manage comfortably, with your back leg underneath your buttocks and your front leg pushing against the wall. By pressing against the rock with, say, the left leg, you can free the right leg, placing it just above the left leg on the facing wall (both feet are temporarily on the same wall). While pressing with the right leg, put the other leg behind your buttocks and achieve a new scissors position. Stand up out of the scissors position, press your back against the wall, and reset your legs into a new scissors position.

Wide Chimneys. These are cracks so wide that you can't effectively place your back against one side of the chimney anymore. If you do, your foot won't reach the other side. This demands a stem or bridge position, whereby you put a hand and a foot against each wall, each limb pressing directly out, counterpressuring against each other.

Chimneying

Now lean over toward the side of the foot you want to lift. Place both hands against the wall on that side, lift the foot on that side with both hands, and slide it up a few inches. Now shift your weight and move your hands to the other side and slide the other foot up. Keep pivoting back and forth in that manner, stemming the whole way.

Stemming is the most efficient way to climb inside corners and wide chimneys. Even if the technique is not used to make progress, it may be the best way to gain a rest; a foot thrown out to create a bridge will allow your weight to rest on your legs, relieving one or both arms.

If a chimney is so wide that your feet can't reach both sides, you are left with only one possible technique, a strenuous one. You must put both feet on one side of the chimney and both hands on the other side and simply walk up the wall, alternating hands and feet. Because your torso is absolutely horizontal, this method demands great flexibility and strength. It's like doing a handstand with someone pushing on the bottoms of your feet.

Laybacking

Sometimes a crack may be impossible to jam. Usually it's a dihedral or a flake that offers either no jams or ones that are too technically difficult, but it could also be straight in. If that happens, you may be left with a technique called *laybacking*, which is basically what someone climbing a palm tree would do.

In laybacking, you pull with your arms while you push with your feet to create opposing pressure against opposite sides of the crack. First grab the lip of the crack and then bring your feet up and push straight into the rock. Get those feet up pretty high, but not too high. If they're too high, you put too much tension on your arms, and you won't be able to hold the position; if they're too low, however, they'll want to slip out. Find a comfortable middle position and move one limb at a time. Don't attempt big moves during a layback. You won't be doing a lot of searching for holds; rather, you're just shuffling up the crack.

Laybacking is straightforward and technically easy, but strenuous. You also may find it difficult to switch from laybacking to jamming. Nevertheless, it is an effective technique for climbing unjammable sections of rock.

Laybacking

Manteling

Manteling is usually used to pull up onto a ledge when no reachable handholds are available. First, use your arms to pull up chest high. Second, lock off with one arm and place the heel of the other hand on the ledge, with the fingers pointing inward toward the other hand and the chest. Then cock the elbow up into a vertical position, as though you were going to support your weight with that arm. Now do the same thing with the other arm, so that both elbows are cocked up, then push up with both arms and straighten them—much like doing a dip on the parallel bars. Carefully bring one foot up, squat, and transfer your weight onto that foot. Balance yourself and press up to a standing position to complete the move. In extreme cases, you may have to do a one-arm mantle, which, although more strenuous, follows the same steps as a two-arm mantle.

Foot Techniques

Proper foot techniques are every bit as important as proper hand techniques. Slab climbing generally requires smearing techniques, vertical climbing requires edging techniques, and overhang climbing requires techniques that use creative positioning of the feet. There also are other creative ways to use your feet, such as heel hooking.

Edging. In this technique, a climber butts the edge of his boot onto a rock edge. Imagine that you're trying to stand on a miniature shelf with an edge of your boot—the front edge, the inside edge by the big toe, the outside edge, or even the heel.

Smearing. Smearing is used on slopes that lack definite edges. Place your foot on the part of the rock that slopes the least, laying as much sole rubber onto the rock as possible. Distribute your weight over as much surface area of the boot as you can. Now you're smearing.

Of course, this technique isn't really new to you. You are smearing in everyday life when you walk up a slight hill. It's really just a matter of spreading your weight over a large area and making maximum use of the static friction created by the sole against the rock.

Heel Hooking. A rare but sometimes effective technique is the heel hook. You can sometimes use heel hooks on larger holds,

Manteling

maneuvering the leg almost as a third arm. A similar technique is the toe hook. On overhangs, you may find yourself using a toe pull in which you use the toe of your boot in a manner similar to the way you would use your fingers in an upward pull.

There may be times when you can get only one foot on a hold. It may be advantageous to leave the other foot dangling, or you can use what's called a *rand smear,* where you push into the side of the rock with the side of the boot. As you can see, there are many creative ways of practicing footwork.

KNOTS

The cave environment, which may feature flowing water or slippery mud, demands reliable knots. They should be strong, easy to identify as correctly tied, and easy to untie. Even the most advanced rigging problems can be handled with a few basic knots.

To keep the stress off the knot, you should employ what is called tensionless rigging. For example, if a tree is used as an anchor, pass the rope around the tree a few times, and then form a loop in the end by tying a figure eight. Clip a carabiner into the loop and clip back

Tensionless rigging

into the main rope. Thanks to this rigging and the friction created by the rope wraps around the tree, the knot should not be subjected to any stress. If the anchor is at all questionable, rig a second anchor strong enough to hold the entire load should the primary anchor fail.

There are several basic knots used in caving. The advantage of knots over more permanent ways of joining ropes and cords together, such as sewn slings, is that knots can be easily untied and retied. The disadvantage is that they force bends in the rope that weaken it. Using knots repeatedly in the same place will produce uneven rope strain, so check regularly for wear.

The following are some important knots in caving:

Figure-Eight Knot

1. Make a bight, passing the loop behind the static part of the rope.
2. Pass the end over the near side and through the loop.
3. Draw the knot tight.
4. Finish off with a half hitch.

A figure-eight knot can be used as a stopper knot on the end of a rope, for tying two ropes together, or for tying into your climbing harness.

Bowline Knot

1. Make a loop in the rope.
2. Pass the tail up through the loop.
3. Pass the tail around behind the static rope and back through the loop.
4. Complete the loop by tying a half hitch on the end; this will prevent slipping.

A bowline can also be used to tie your rope to your climbing harness. Avoid a three-way pull on this knot, as that may untie it.

FALLING

The best advice is, don't fall. The consequences of an underground fall tend to be much more dire than one aboveground. Because of those dangers, vertical cavers are less likely to fall than horizontal

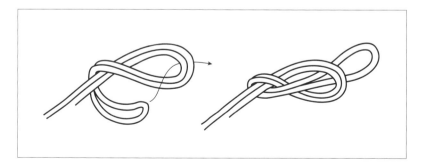

Figure-eight knot

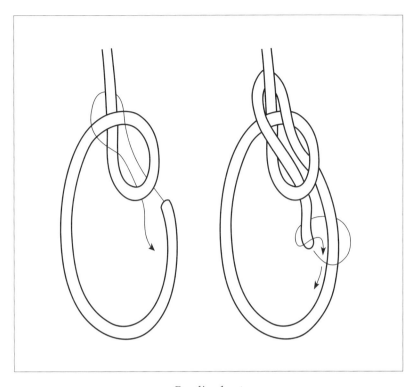

Bowline knot

explorers. You can be seriously injured tripping on nonvertical rock, flipping upside down, and hitting your head. Your best defense there is to be careful and wear a helmet.

You have to play a delicate mental game regarding falling. On the one hand, you should know what you will hit if you do fall; on the other hand, you don't want to dwell on the possibility so much that it distracts you and actually causes a fall. What's most important is to be ready for the unexpected.

7

Discovering New Caves

Every sport has its cutting edge, its supreme symbol of success. For baseball players, it's the Major Leagues; for bicyclists, the Olympics or the Tour de France. Ice climbers push the envelope by scaling ever thinner ice. For cavers, the ultimate goal is to discover a new cave, or a new part of a known cave.

Let's say you've worked your way through a thorough apprenticeship. You've explored commercial caverns, a variety of horizontal caves, maybe even done some vertical caving. You are now ready to become an explorer, to go where others have not gone before you. You have undertaken quite a challenge. If you are to have any chance of success, you must put in hours of study and fieldwork. Why would you make such an investment? Because there are few moments in life as thrilling, as gratifying, as breath-expelling as discovering a new cave.

WHERE TO LOOK

Discounting glacial caves, which are beyond the focus of this book, the vast majority of caves are found in limestone, with maybe 10 percent forming as lava tubes. Limestone is deposited either in broad beds or in large, discrete chunks, called pods or lenses. Caves tend to proliferate in a type of limestone that is dense, fractures easily, and has been in contact with a lot of water.

HOW TO LOOK

Become a private investigator and start poking around local libraries, historical societies, newspaper offices, and country recorders. Talk to old-timers who might have heard of caves in their youth. Ask commercial cavern owners or guides about possible wild caves nearby. The presence of known caves increases the chances of finding others in the neighborhood. Also inquire of local farmers, hunters, fishermen, miners, and owners of land that might harbor caves.

TOPOGRAPHIC MAPS

Acquire topographic maps of your local caving area from the nearest camping store. Topos, as they are called, are used by most cavers to find their way to caves, discover areas likely to contain new caves, and pinpoint the location of caves for fellow cavers.

At first glance, a topographic map looks like an incomprehensible jumble of squiggly lines, but it's really quite legible. Here's a way to make sense of it. Imagine that you place an ice cream cone upside down on a piece of paper. Your task is to draw a topo map of sugar cone mountain that will depict its cone shape if you are looking straight down on it.

Draw a line around the base of the cone. That circle is the outside perimeter of the mountain. Any point on that line is the same elevation as any other point on that line. Now measure all around the cone 1 inch up from the table and slice the cone along that line. Put the partial cone back on the paper and draw around the new base. You now have a circle within a circle. The inside circle represents all the points on the cone exactly 1 inch up from the table.

If you repeated the process, each time measuring another inch up from the table, you would wind up with multiple concentric circles. Those lines are the equivalent of the *contour lines* on a topo map. Contour lines connect points of equal elevation, so they never touch or overlap. You gain or lose elevation when you travel from one line to another.

Now let's add a topographic feature to this symmetrical cone. Imagine pressing in slowly near the bottom of one side of the slope to create a small valley. If you were to look down at the cone from directly overhead, the contours of the valley would form V's, with the tips pointing uphill. Sometimes the V's are softened into U's, but the principle remains the same.

Note that if you create two adjacent valleys, you also create a spur ridge between them. Spur contours resemble valley contours, except that spur contours are generally U-shaped and point downward.

How do you tell the difference between a valley and a spur? The presence of a blue line indicating a stream is a sure sign of a valley. In the absence of a stream, compare the elevations of the contours to determine which way the land is sloping.

Back at sugar cone mountain, note that the spacing of the circles is constant, because a cone's sides slope at a constant rate all the way around. But what if the cone were asymmetrical? The accompanying diagram illustrates the following points to help you make sense of topo maps:

- In addition to regular contour lines, there are index contours and form lines. The bold contours are called *index contours;* every fifth contour is an index contour, with its elevation noted periodically along its length. *Form lines* are broken contours at approximately one-half interval, used when necessary to show the shape of the land.

- The vertical distance between contour lines, known as the *contour interval,* is always given. If the contour interval is 5 meters, you climb or drop 5 meters if you travel from one line to the next. The larger the contour interval, usually the less detailed the map. The contour interval varies from map to map but is always the same on a given map. A map of the flatlands of Florida might use a contour interval of 2.5 meters; for the Rocky Mountains, it might be 30 meters. It would not do to use a 30-meter contour interval in Florida, where the highest point is 345 feet above sea level; with so few contour lines, the map would not be very informative. Conversely, a 2.5-meter contour interval in mountainous terrain would bunch the lines so severely as to render them unreadable.

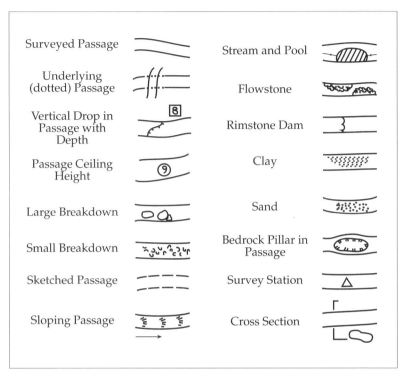

Surveyed Passage		Stream and Pool	
Underlying (dotted) Passage		Flowstone	
Vertical Drop in Passage with Depth		Rimstone Dam	
Passage Ceiling Height		Clay	
Large Breakdown		Sand	
Small Breakdown		Bedrock Pillar in Passage	
Sketched Passage		Survey Station	
Sloping Passage		Cross Section	

Topographic map symbols

- To calculate your gain or loss of elevation, count the number of contour lines you cross and multiple by the contour interval. For example, if the contour interval is 10 meters and your route up the mountain crosses nine lines, you have gained approximately 90 vertical meters.
- Lines close to one another indicate steep terrain—an abrupt drop, falls, or a canyon—and lines far apart show a gradual change in elevation. Because a vertical cliff has elevation change over nearly zero horizontal distance, mapmakers depict such cliffs with contour lines that merge.
- Walk along a single contour line and you remain at the same elevation.

- The closed end of contour V's point upstream.
- U-shaped contours indicate a spur. The closed ends of the U's point downhill.
- The actual height of many objects, such as hilltops or trail junctions, is often noted, sometimes with a dot.

Here's a good way to mark the caves you already know on your topos. Make a pinhole at the exact location. Then on the back, where there's plenty of room, circle each hole and write the cave's name and other relevant data. By holding the map up to the light, you will be able to see the holes.

GEOLOGIC MAPS

Geologic maps, which are found in the reports of the U.S. Geologic Survey and state mineral resource agencies, and in university geology department theses, can be an invaluable aid for cavers.

Geologic maps use colors or patterns to identify the kinds of rocks that lie just beneath the topsoil. If the map is detailed enough, sedimentary rocks like limestone and igneous rocks like lava will have their own color or pattern. And as we now know, limestone from the Paleozoic age (about 300 million years ago) is the most common cave-bearing rock. Limestone is usually shown in blue. In the most detailed maps, limestone and marble (metamorphic limestone) will be separately identified as l and m. Look also for rock that, although dominated by some other type, contains some limestone.

Rock boundaries are not precise on geologic maps. When you're out hunting for caves, expand your search beyond the indicated limestone boundaries. Correct your personal map as needed.

AERIAL PHOTOGRAPHS

Once you've isolated a possible cave area, aerial photographs can provide important additional information. They are expensive to have made, but the local library or college geology department may have them available for your perusal. Studying an aerial photo with a stereoscopic tabletop viewer really makes the hills and depressions jump out at you.

IN THE FIELD

Let's say you've targeted a broad area of limestone as having possible caves. You and your partners have used your topo map and compass to reach that location. Now pick a relatively small area and focus on it. Most limestone cave entrances are either *solution* or *collapse* in origin.

Solution caves were formed by water eating away at limestone, so follow the water trail. Ask key questions to direct your search: Where are the drainages? Where does the water flow into and out of the hills? Look for springs, sinkholes, and streams disappearing underground. An entrance often may be found at the bottom of a sinkhole, near or at the bottom of a gully, or on the side of a valley or canyon. Solution sinkholes, usually bowl shaped with smooth sides, are often found along a line between where a stream sinks and resurfaces. Keep in mind that the size of the swallow hole is not necessarily a good indicator of the size of the cave below.

Collapse entrances are harder to predict, as they may have been formed by water-flow patterns that are now ancient history. Collapse sinkholes have steep walls and may be almost any shape. They too tend to be on a line between stream disappearance and resurgence. Look for other collapse entrances on the side or at the base of escarpments, where a cave entrance may have been obscured by a landslide.

Limestone Outcroppings

In an area of limestone outcroppings, investigate cracks and small openings that have air blowing out of them. This air can be steamily visible in the winter, when midlatitude caves are normally warmer than the outside air. Look for melted snow at cave entrances.

Karst

Another clue that there may be caves is the presence of few surface streams in an area of copious rainfall. This usually means that surface streams dive quickly underground and flow through subterranean

SAMPLE RELEASE

I, the undersigned, do hereby release _____

_____ ,
its officers, agents or servants or others from any and all liability, claims, demands, actions, and causes of action whatso-
ever, arising out of or relating to any loss, damage, or injury,
including death, that may be sustained by the undersigned
while at or en route to or from any expedition or project under
supervision by or in connection with caving.

The undersigned being duly aware of the risks and hazards
inherent in caving or in participation in caving, does hereby
elect voluntarily to participate knowing of said dangers.

This release shall be binding upon the distributees, heirs,
next-of-kin, executors, and administrators of the undersigned
and is given in consideration of the undersigned being
allowed to participate in caving activities in which the
released entities above are involved.

In WITNESS WHEREOF, the undersigned has hereto voluntarily affixed his signature.

Date	Name	Address	Telephone

Sample release form

SAMPLE RELEASE AND WAIVER

(county), (state)
(date)

In consideration of the granting of permission to
_____ to enter upon premises known
as _____ located at
_____ , and owned or controlled
by _____ , for the purpose
of exploring underground holes, caves, crevices, and passageways, the undersigned acknowledges that such exploration
may be inherently dangerous and assumes all risks, known
and unknown, which may arise from such exploration and
hereby waives any and all losses, claims, or liabilities which I
or my heirs may have for any and all losses and damage
which may occur to my person or property while engaged in
such exploration and further do hereby release and hold harmless the owner, _____ , agents
and employees, and heirs from such claims or liabilities.

I have read this release and understand all its terms. I exe-
cute it voluntarily and with full knowledge of its significance.

_____
(signature)
(Parent or Guardian, if minor)

Sample release form

White crusts in a Hawaiian lava tube

channels in the limestone or gypsum. This kind of terrain, sculpted by acidic water dissolving rock and characterized by sinkholes, subterranean drainage, and caves, is called *karst.* The sinkholes may not be obvious from the surface, but from an airplane or nearby hill, they usually stand out.

The Dig

If you find strong indications of a cave but no entrance and you wish to pursue it, first check with the landowner and get permission to proceed. Have the owner sign a waiver. If surface digging is required, fence off the area to protect people and animals from falling into your hole. Many caves have been discovered by digging, but this activity has its own unique hazards. If the dig is going to be very deep, you must shore up the sides of the tunnel to prevent collapse. Carefully consider the consequences before using dynamite to unearth a possible cave. Talk to local cavers and other residents. Besides being dangerous, blasting is environmentally unfriendly. If blasting is absolutely necessary, seek the services of a licensed professional.

NEW WINGS OF OLD CAVES

Almost as satisfying as discovering a new cave is discovering a new passage in an old cave. Many large caves were discovered piecemeal. Mammoth Cave system, the world's longest, grows with each new discovery of a connecting passage.

When seeking new passages within an existing cave, look for areas filled with dirt or large breakdown blocks. Excavation may expose more cave. Mud or breakdown may signal past flooding or the collapse of a roof, and the passage may continue on the other side.

A surface survey can sometimes turn up important clues, especially if it can be coordinated with a good map of the cave.

LAVA TUBES

Lava tubes are prolific in areas of relatively recent volcanic activity, such as the western United States and Hawaii. They are formed when the outer surface of the lava flow cools and hardens before its molten interior, which continues to flow until empty. Tubes form only in a smooth type of lava called *pahoehoe* (a Hawaiian term, pronounced "pa-hoy-hoy") and not in the jagged type called *aa* (meaning "hurtful to the bare feet").

When the roof of a tube collapses, an entrance is created. In the winter, steam plumes may emanate from that entrance. The collapse may be due to natural or man-made causes, including road crews and loggers. For this reason, you can find many cave entrances near recently constructed roads and in logging areas. Aerial photos often reveal the existence and direction of lava flows.

> My hair stood on end, my teeth chattered, my lips trembled.
> —Jules Verne,
> *Journey to the Center of the Earth*

8

Health and Safety

After reading the harrowing tale of Floyd Collins, you might be inclined to stay out of caves forever. But Collins's ordeal occurred seventy years ago, and he made some basic errors that you won't make after you've read this chapter.

Caving is not as dangerous as most people think. Sports that are far riskier, such as motorcycling and skiing, are taken for granted. Good training, technique, and equipment will overcome most cave hazards. Statistically, the most dangerous part of the trip is the drive to the site.

CAVER SAFETY QUIZ

1. Do you always have permission from the landowner to enter the cave?
2. Do you always leave your exact whereabouts and anticipated time out of a cave with a responsible person?
3. Do you know if any other members in your group have any caving or first-aid experience?
4. Do you use a good-quality helmet?

continued

---

5. Do you use either a carbide or an electric headlamp and two backup lights?
6. Do you carry a small first-aid kit?
7. Have you ever had any first-aid training?
8. Have you had formal training in ropework?
9. Do you know what a heat tent is?
10. Could you stay comfortable all night in a cave if you became lost?
11. Would you recognize the signs of hypothermia?

If you answered no to any of the above questions, you should avail yourself of modern safety techniques, lest you wind up needing a rescue.

PREPARATION

Careful planning and preparation are the keys to a safe caving trip. The National Speleological Society urges you to take at least the following steps before you even reach the entrance:

- Learn the limitations of the members of your group. You should be aware of each person's experience, fitness level, medical condition, and any other factors that might influence caving performance.
- Make sure everyone has proper safety equipment in good condition and enough food and water for an unexpected stay in the cave.
- Make sure a responsible person knows exactly where you are going and when you plan to return. That person should know who to call if you are overdue.
- Make sure your group understands, and is committed to, conservation ethics.
- Consider "what ifs," discussing various scenarios—becoming lost, injured, trapped by flood—and how to respond.

- Know the limitations of the cave you intend to explore. Each cave is unique, with its own special conditions and hazards. Some may include rockfall, flash floods, vertical drops, bad air, and airborne diseases.
- Obtain a cave map, if available.
- Obtain permission to enter from the managing agency or cave owner.
- Avoid caves too technically difficult for your skill level.

ATTITUDE

A good caver sets out not to conquer a cave but to explore it, using equipment designed to make the task easier, all the while avoiding hazards and damage to the cave. If you're part of a team, be a team player. Be guided by the two C's: care and cooperation. The inside of a cave is not the time for macho posturing.

On the other hand, don't go overboard worrying over subterranean threats, lest you lose your perspective. Caving is usually quite safe; however, if something does go wrong, you should know what to do and be prepared to do it.

LEAVING WORD

Floyd Collins did do one thing right: He made sure someone knew where he was. Always tell a responsible person—family member, fellow caver, or friend—where you are going and when you plan to be back. Include the name of the cave and the precise section you intend to explore. Add a few hours of cushion to your anticipated exit time to allow for unforeseen events and prevent unnecessary rescue attempts.

Leave word with the cave owner or caretaker, if any. If you have standing permission to enter a cave and no one is around, leave a note with sufficient detail. Include contingency plans in case weather or conditions change.

GO AS A TEAM

Four cavers in a party is a safe minimum, especially for beginners. If a caver is incapacitated, one companion can stay with the victim and two can go for help. If the individual cavers are experienced, two or three may explore a known cave.

To avoid a predicament such as Floyd Collins's, never cave alone. To the solitary caver, a relatively minor incident—a sprained ankle, failing light, a fall into a stream—becomes a major problem.

Move in single file, for both safety and conservation purposes. The leader or most experienced person should go first, the novices in the middle, and the second most experienced at the end. Single file allows everyone close contact with at least one other person and makes it easy to pass messages back and forth. Avoid constant chatter and yelling, so that messages can be heard and everyone's attention stays focused on balanced movement.

Even though you are moving as a team, you can't rely on someone else to be aware for you. As a party moves through a cave, each individual caver should be posing the same questions, at least to themselves: "Did we leave the rope properly placed after rappel?" "Is that loose rock up ahead?" "Are these the best hand- and footholds?"

Keep your senses revved to the maximum in order to anticipate and identify potential hazards. Hazards include not only those near you, but those near your partners, too. If you lack total concentration, slow down until you regain it. You will enjoy the cave more that way anyway.

To evaluate hazards, you must consider the limitations of each member of your party. What's safe for you may not be for someone else, and vice versa. For example, a move that's easy for someone with long arms and a low center of gravity may not be easy for someone with weak arms and a high center of gravity.

Take fewer risks as you move farther from the entrance. Make decisions that produce progressively less serious consequences. A sprained ankle, a minor inconvenience near a horizontal entrance, may force a major rescue if it happens at the bottom of a deep pit. One defense you always have is to turn back.

ENTERING A NEW CAVE

Discovering a new, possibly untrammeled cave can be thrilling—and disorienting. First and foremost, maintain your cool. Second, be extra

> Because good cavers prepare well and are supersensitive to their surroundings, many of them have caved for years with no serious injuries. Dick Graham, writing in *The Groundhog*, a grotto newsletter, says: "I have been caving for 25 years in a variety of caves, and I have never had an injury causing more than temporary, minor pain. . . . Most of the experienced cavers I cave with have never had a serious injury. But I have sprained an ankle four times outside of a cave—once while walking across a smooth street."

vigilant. It's easy to be distracted by virgin speleothems, but unvisited passages may have unstable rocks that demand your attention. Stop to admire the sights. When you move, do it slowly and quietly. Beware of thin calcite floors under which the dirt has eroded—they may be false floors several feet above the real floor.

LOST AND FOUND

Getting seriously lost is hard in most caves, though many cavers will admit to occasional disorientation, especially in complex cave systems. Old-timers used to carry string into caves, in the manner of Tom Sawyer, but they eventually discovered that it's difficult to get lost in a cave small enough to require only an average-size ball of string. Larger caves, where it is possible to get lost, take more string than one group can easily carry.

A simple but effective way to keep track of your route is to turn around regularly and note what the passage looks like going the other way. Stop and look back at every junction, especially those where several passages meet. Stay alert to what lies ahead, too. Pay special attention to distinctive passage shapes, speleothems, and other features that can be identified on the return trip.

If the entire group gets lost, it may be time to stop and "take five." Send someone up ahead and someone else back down the passage to see what looks familiar. Discuss your situation as a group, letting your collective memory chew on the problem.

If you get separated from the group, stifle the urge to panic. Instead of running around aimlessly, which will wear you out and probably worsen your position, sit for a moment and collect your thoughts. Yell to your comrades periodically; the intertwining passages may allow them to hear you even though you can't hear them. If you stay put or simply return to your last known location, you will increase your chances of being found.

If help does not arrive in a few minutes and you feel you must move on, look for obvious signs of human traffic in the passages. These might include footprints, survey markers, "out" arrows, and unfortunately, trash. Be careful, though, that these clues lead you out and not deeper into difficult areas of the cave. Normally, arrows smoked on cave walls with carbide lamps point *out* of the cave. Although not a recommended practice anymore, they can still be seen in some well-traveled passages.

When lost and confronting multiple passages, leave a person, candle, or other marker behind to identify the return route. Don't leave behind your pack; you never know when you may need the spare light you have stashed there.

ACCIDENTS

Drowning
Most caves have standing, flowing, or dripping water—after all, they were sculpted by water. The type and severity of hazard created by cave water vary, depending on the amount of water in the cave, the local topography, temperature, and amount of precipitation.

Even experienced cavers can have trouble predicting when caves will flood, as it depends on so many factors, including direction and intensity of rainfall, size of catchment draining into the cave, soil saturation level, and angle of subterranean passages. Some caves flood so quickly that they are safe only in the coldest winter weather, when the surface water is frozen. When the weather warms, flooding may be caused by melting snow or by intense rainfall onto impermeable ice.

> Because of the poor lighting in caves, streams and pools are often deeper than they look.

Many caves are located in hilly or mountainous country, with a thin soil covering, steep slopes, and relatively little vegetation to intercept rainfall. Upland streams that flow across impervious rock can swell quickly after the onset of rain or snowmelt, flooding any cave in the stream's path. If the surface above the cave is typical karst limestone, it is usually bare of soil or vegetation, allowing rainwater to run freely down every crack and flood underground waterways. For unwary cavers lacking surface clues, a cave may go from trickle to raging torrent faster than you can say "scuba gear." Sometimes normally dry passages, well above the level of permanent streams, can become flood overflow channels with no warning. When rushing water meets a constriction, it will back up, sometimes filling the cave behind to amazing depths. In dry weather, a French cave, Grotte de la Luire, allows cavers to descend vertically for more than 1,500 feet; yet during downpours, flood water may pour from its entrance. Following such an onslaught, especially during the dry season, cave streams may diminish to mere trickles or dry up altogether, allowing cavers to penetrate areas that were impassable a short time before.

If a cave system is going to respond to rainfall, it will often do it a few hours or less after the start of a downpour. Summer thunderstorms can be particularly troublesome. They tend to occur near the end of a period of high pressure. The weather has been fine and the water levels low, tempting cavers to extend their exploration. The morning dawns clear and the caving trip begins with little thought to the weather. But by early afternoon, surface dwellers begin to hear the distant rumbling of thunder. This is followed by a relentless buildup of dark cumulus clouds and then rain, often intense. Other things being equal, the heavier the rain, the quicker the flood, and sometimes caves can flood in minutes instead of hours.

Determine the flood risks of the cave you plan to visit by reading guidebooks and, whenever possible, soliciting local knowledge. Some caves are high risk; others never flood. If there is any flood risk, obtain the last possible weather forecast before departure.

Novices should avoid caves with a steep sinkhole entrance, an active stream running through the entrance, or leaves and branches caught high up on rock ledges. Be especially wary when the weather (or the prediction) looks bad, or when it has rained hard in the past few hours or days (the flood waters may just be reaching your cave).

Once inside a cave, look for signs of past flooding, such as mud, tide marks, the absence of delicate formations, and washed-in vegetation high on the walls. Be alert to changes in air movement; rising waters; or an increase in noise from streams, mud and debris in the water, or foam at the base of a waterfall.

When you spot any of these warning signs, act quickly and calmly. If you are just entering an area with rising water hazards and there are no streams behind you, the safest option is to turn around. On the other hand, if the cave has an active stream flowing through its entrance or if there are other water hazards between you and the entrance, it may be better to take refuge in an upper passage above the apparent flood line. The water may take a few hours to recede, so get comfortable and conserve your light.

Whenever possible, rig your pitches away from potential flood water. This is usually done by starting the pitch with a traverse, which will carry you above or around the corner from falling water.

If you get caught by a sudden rush of water, try to escape to the highest point available. Huddle with others for warmth, use your emergency bag, conserve food and strength, and stay clear of drafty places, such as the bottom of pitches.

At times, a rubber dinghy will be the best way to cross a short section of deep water. Unless it can be pulled forward and backward by rope, it must be large enough to hold at least two cavers so that everyone can be ferried across. Take care to avoid punctures on sharp limestone. Consider using Ping-Pong paddles, which are smaller and lighter than normal raft paddles.

Sometimes the water in a cave passage is nearly to the roof. Called a *duck,* this situation demands great care. In order to breathe, you may have to turn your head to one side, as you do during the crawl stroke, or lie on your back so that your nostrils are out of the water. If it's a short duck, you may be able to get through by holding your breath. Whichever method you use, stay calm; this is no time to panic.

If the cave entrance is mostly underwater, you should be prepared to swim it. Make sure that every member of the party is aided by a wetsuit, a life jacket, or a handline. Even strong swimmers have been dragged down by the weight of their equipment, and deep water may have dangerous currents or obstructions. This is not an activity for beginners.

A passage filled with water right to the roof is called a *sump.* If the passage is short and familiar, you may be able to hold your breath and free-dive it. Sometimes a rope will be in place to guide you; it can also be a way of signaling via tugs. You should have considerable experience before attempting free dives of unfamiliar passages longer than about 6 feet.

Cave-diving sumps with scuba gear, a growing sport in its own right, is beyond the scope of this book, although it is briefly discussed later in this chapter. Suffice it to say, cave divers should be proficient divers as well as experienced cavers. Join a cave-diving group and learn from experienced members.

The two basic rules of sumps:
- Never attempt to free-dive an unknown sump.
- Always have someone along who knows the sump and can guide the others.

Breathing Bad Air

Unlike mines, where oxygen-deficient air is common, most caves have good air circulation. A 1975 study concluded that less than 1 percent of caves have bad air. Indeed, the air in most caves is so pure that they have long been used as therapeutic havens for patients with lung disorders. In the rare instances when cave air has gone bad, it is almost always due to an excessive buildup of carbon dioxide.

Be especially cautious in small, heavily traveled passages and in small air bells between two sumps. Bad air can be found in caves harboring large quantities of decaying vegetation, near thermal springs with high levels of carbon dioxide or hydrogen sulfide, or near gasoline or chemical storage tanks. Local cavers should be able to tell you about any locales with bad air.

If anyone in your group becomes unaccountably short of breath, find the nearest exit. The effects of poisoned air can be swift and deadly. It's a myth that a candle is an effective test of air quality. In many cases, a candle will outlast a fit person.

Burns

Here's accident rule number one: Never light a fire underground. Besides consuming oxygen, releasing deadly carbon dioxide, and polluting the cave, it also could ignite bat guano, which is not only flammable but explosive. If hot food is a necessity, cook on canned heat or a small backpacking stove in a well-ventilated area.

The flame of a carbide lamp can also cause serious burns. If the base of the lamp is not screwed on tight or a poor gasket is used, gas can escape around the bottom and burst into flames.

EQUIPMENT HAZARDS

Equipment failure when caving is a safety issue. Check your gear before you leave home, and know its limitations. Test even new equipment under caving conditions. Dick Graham, a caver from Huntsville, Alabama, has had to rescue novices who entered vertical caves by sliding down wire or clothesline, only to discover they couldn't slide back up. "It would have been a simple matter for them to have tried climbing hand-over-hand in a tree before attempting a pit and causing so many people grief," says Graham.

You're only as safe as the equipment you use, so don't rely on old wooden ladders or natural-fiber ropes (manila, hemp, or sisal) that have been left behind in caves. The high humidity of caves is hard on these materials. Bolts left by previous parties should also be treated with extreme caution unless you know their history. Even then, test before using them as anchors.

Try to avoid leaving behind ladders or rigging; this invites accidents as well as liability problems. For that reason, the National Speleological Society recommends the removal of old vertical equipment.

Ask the important questions about your equipment, even if it's new: Can you use your new light effectively? Does it point in the right direction? Will it stay on your hard hat? How many hours do those batteries have left? Will your electric light dim gradually or extinguish completely when the batteries wear down? Will your pack fall apart in the first crawlway? If it does, how will you carry your gear? How much will it slow you down? If a particular item fails, how much more strenuous will the trip be? How much more difficult will the climbs be? Will your clothing keep you warm if you have to wade through pools of water? Does the food you brought agree with your stomach? Is your rope long enough? Is it suitable for rappelling? These questions, and others, should be asked and answered *before* you enter a cave.

The trend in caving is increasingly toward packing light so that you can go fast and far. It thus becomes even more important to consider each piece of equipment for safety. Some items are essential. No serious caver ever ventures underground without a high-quality, impact-resistant hard hat, complete with quick-release chin strap and lamp. At least two backup sources of light are a must, typically an extra carbide or electric lamp, chemical light sticks, or flashlights. Include fuel and parts for all light sources. If a flashlight is used as a backup, carry spare dry cells and bulbs. Ordinary carbon-zinc dry cells should not be used for caving, as they have a short shelf life and a limited capacity; the alkaline variety hold their charge much longer.

Candles used to be the universal choice for a third light source, but they are inadequate unless you are stationary; when you're moving, they are hard to keep lit.

Find out where first-aid training is available in your area, and encourage members of your group to enroll and learn essential lifesaving skills. First-aid courses are available through the American Red Cross and Emergency Medical Technician programs.

EMERGENCY GEAR

The practical long-range planner will pack extra gear to handle a variety of emergencies. Beginners often carry insufficient clothing and food, which can hasten hypothermia. Besides standard clothing, consider bringing space blankets, garbage bags, candles, waterproof matches, and a balaclava. A flame placed under a space blanket or garbage bag spread out like an awning can produce quite a bit of heat.

Also take first-aid items (see chapter 3); extra gear for vertical rescue, including a hammer (to enlarge passages); extra rope; and change for a couple of phone calls. If you require special medication, be sure to have it with you and inform the other members of your group of this fact.

Package the first-aid items in a waterproof container. If you cannot fit all of the extra equipment in packs, prioritize items on the basis of the likelihood of particular emergencies. If you can't carry

A piece of equipment that can be useful in a pinch is a length of 1-inch tubular webbing 30 to 50 feet long. Webbing packs smaller than rope and is easier to grip. Use it as a belay for less experienced cavers, as a guideline on a slippery ledge, or as an aid in rigging a rope to irregular projections. The best tubular webbing has a continuous circular stitch; the kind made by folding a 2-inch piece and fastening with a chain stitch is weaker and less durable.

into the cave all the emergency gear you think you may need, you should at least have it near the entrance or in your car.

DISEASE HAZARDS AND PHYSICAL DISORDERS
Rabies

First, the good news for cavers: Between 1980 and 1993 only eighteen people died of rabies in the United States, and ten of those victims became infected in other countries. The worst carriers of the disease are raccoons and skunks, neither of which hangs out in caves.

Now the bad news: The threat of rabies is rising, the disease is usually fatal to humans, bats rank fourth on the list of carriers, and at least two victims contracted rabies by breathing virus-laden air in caves with dense bat populations. Still, only a tiny percentage of bats is infected, and very few cavers ever come down with the disease. Although bats are often reviled by humans, they are ecologically beneficial and usually harmless. Some species consume vast quantities of insects. And bat guano is a key part of the food chain in most caves.

As your first line of defense against rabies, make it a habit to enjoy wildlife from a distance. Never handle any bat, especially one lying on the floor (it could be sick). Be alert for poorly circulating air that reeks of ammonia, a by-product of decaying guano. When confronted with a wild animal behaving unnaturally (look for aggressive behavior and loss of coordination), resist the impulse to help, and notify the authorities. If bitten or otherwise exposed to the rabies virus, immediately wash the wound with soap and water and then seek medical help.

If you plan to visit caves that house huge bat colonies, seek information and advice from local cavers and public health officials. If rabid bats have been reported, consider preexposure immunization. Side effects are minimal. Protection, which lasts for one to two years, is easily confirmed by a test. You can achieve more or less permanent immunity by getting regular booster shots.

Histoplasmosis

Histoplasmosis is a disease with flulike symptoms caused by a pathogenic fungus, *Histoplasma capsulatum.* The fungus grows in moist soil, mostly in the tropics, but occasionally in temperate latitudes, where it produces spores. The spores are carried by the wind, and if they are inhaled by warm-blooded animals, they produce yeast cells in the lungs, which cause the disease.

Bats can become infected by inhaling the spores, and the fungus can be released in the bats' feces. Thus, some bat caves are repositories of *H. capsulatum.* After a few well-publicized cases where every member of a caving party contracted histoplasmosis after a visit to a particular cave, the disease was labeled in some circles "cave fever." In fact, relatively few people contract histoplasmosis in caves. Cases are more commonly associated with soil contaminated by birds. Some people have contracted the disease in caves after breathing heavy cave dust generated by digging in guano. If you are visiting a very dusty cave or otherwise will be exposed to cave dust, infected or not, you would be wise to wear a face mask.

Symptoms range from almost none to flulike for one to four days. In a rare and extreme form of the disease, the infected cells may be carried in the bloodstream to organs, where they may proliferate, killing the victim. More severe infections are often mistaken for atypical pneumonia, with a cough, mild chest pains, and fever.

Histoplasmosis is most common in the central part of the United States, including the Ohio and Mississippi Valleys, and along the Mexican border. Thus, histoplasmosis is present in some of America's prime caving country. Still, the odds of a caver contracting this disease are pretty remote, and if he does, the symptoms will likely be mild. Exploring a cave known to harbor *H. capsulatum* is not recommended, but otherwise don't let this fungus keep you from your appointed rounds.

Hypothermia

Hypothermia is a dangerous drop in core temperature, whereby the body no longer generates enough heat to keep up with heat loss. You are most susceptible to hypothermia if you are wet, injured, or not moving about enough to stay warm. It can happen in minutes or take hours. It doesn't have to be freezing cold for hypothermia to strike; in fact, it's most common when the temperature is between 30 and 50 degrees F. Far more insidious than temperature are wind and moisture, which can penetrate clothing and remove the insulating layer of warm air next to the body.

Hypothermia is easier to prevent than to treat. Eat well, including high-energy snacks on the trip, drink plenty of fluids, control sweat and fatigue, keep a positive attitude, and dress for the conditions. If you expect to get fully immersed in water, wear a wetsuit. When exploring cold, damp caves, select the proper clothing, starting with polypropylene underwear and adding layers. Pay special attention to the head, neck, hands, and feet, emphasizing clothes that retain their insulative properties even when wet. Whenever you face an otherwise equal choice between a wet passage and a dry one, stay dry, especially on the way into the cave. Water conducts heat away from the body twenty-five times better than air.

Hypothermia is classified as either mild or profound. The difference can be difficult to detect if you don't have a thermometer that reads below 95 degrees F. Mild hypothermia generally involves little loss of mental acuity or walking coordination. The victim may be shivering and may have difficulty managing buttons, zippers, or laces. He may also be lethargic, apathetic, with slow or slurred speech.

Treatment for hypothermia should begin immediately. Insulate the victim from the ground up—that is, have him lie atop clothes or a pack. Remove wet clothing and put on dry. Protect from any further heat loss, especially from the head and neck. Give warm, nonalcoholic beverages. No complications should result from mild hypothermia, and the victim may resume activity when warming is complete.

Profound hypothermia involves a marked change in mental status. The victim may become belligerent or uncooperative and dispute your diagnosis of his condition. Muscle rigidity replaces shivering. Movements become erratic and jerky. Core temperature falls below 95 degrees F. As temperature continues to drop, the victim becomes irrational, loses contact with reality, and falls into a stupor. If untreated, the victim will die from cardiac arrest or other complications.

Treatment for profound hypothermia includes the measures used for the mild form, and more. To accelerate the warming process, place wrapped warm rocks or hot-water bottles around the victim. Treat gently when removing clothing and giving care; sudden movement may force cold blood from the limbs into the core of the body. Do not rub or squeeze the extremities to stimulate circulation—it can damage tissue. If possible, place the victim in a sleeping bag or in between two other people who are nonhypothermic. Continue warming until the victim can be evacuated to a medical facility.

Shock

Shock is the body's response to injury, serious illness, overwhelming blood loss, infection, or dehydration. It happens when the blood supply to the vital organs, the skin, and the muscles is decreased. When the blood flow to the internal organs—intestines, kidneys, heart, and brain—falls far enough, collapse follows. Severe shock leads to death when the heart stops.

The symptoms of shock include pale, cold, and clammy skin; shallow, irregular breathing; rapid but weak pulse; dilated pupils; beads of perspiration; weakness; nausea; and thirst. Loss of consciousness may follow.

Shock signifies an emergency, necessitating immediate medical intervention. Take the following measures:

- Have the patient lie down flat. In case of vomiting, turn the head to one side to prevent aspiration (inhaling vomit into the lungs).
- Loosen any tight clothing, particularly about the head.
- Keep the victim warm, but avoid sweating.
- Speak soothingly, striving to instill confidence in you and in recovery.
- Light, rhythmical massaging is comforting; holding the hands or feet can be reassuring.
- Do not give water if the victim is unconscious, nauseated, or if medical help will arrive within thirty minutes. If medical help is more than thirty minutes away, then give only small sips.
- If the victim stops breathing and the heart stops, cardiopulmonary resuscitation (CPR) should be started immediately.

CPR should be learned by everyone. Classes are available through the American Heart Association and the Red Cross.

Giardiasis

Contaminated water sources are believed to account for most infectious diarrhea in wilderness areas. This is a recent phenomenon. In a 1977 Sierra Club backpacker's guide, the author lauded drinking directly from wilderness water as one of the "very special pleasures" of backcountry travel. No more. Today, primarily because of a protozoan called *Giardia lamblia,* such reckless behavior is a type of wilderness Russian roulette.

Giardia lamblia is a microscopic cyst that causes a parasitic disease called *giardiasis. Giardia* is spread by fecal-oral transmission, meaning the infectious organism is shed in feces that finds it way into water that finds its way into a new host. Giardiasis used to be called "beaver fever," which conveniently misplaced the blame for the problem. Beavers were around long before *Giardia,* and besides, the disease is prevalent in areas alien to beavers. The more likely villains are humans, possibly cross-country skiers who relieve themselves in the snow, which later melts, carrying the parasites into waterways.

In olden times—say, pre-1978—water that looked good and was moving fast was considered safe. Today, according to the Centers for Disease Control in Atlanta, no water on the planet is guaranteed free of *Giardia.* The cysts have been discovered in mountain headwaters. As soon as water falls from the sky, it is technically possible for *Giardia* to be present in it.

Giardiasis is an unpleasant, at times debilitating, disease whose symptoms include chronic diarrhea, commencing about seven to ten days after ingestion, along with abdominal distention, flatulence, and cramping, especially after meals. Symptoms last seven to twenty-one days, followed by periods of relief, then relapses.

Preventing Giardiasis. Outside of caves, away from established toilets, dig an environmentally sound toilet hole 6 to 8 inches deep, well above the high-water line of spring runoff, and far enough from surface water—150 feet is usually recommended—to prevent feces from washing into it. Educate children and newcomers to the wilderness on the need to do the same. Always wash hands after squatting and before handling food.

If possible, use only tap water for drinking. If not possible, carefully boil, treat, or filter your drinking water. Years ago, the only choice was between boiling and chemical treatment, either iodine or chlorine. Both methods have serious drawbacks.

Boiling takes time and fuel and leaves you with hot, flat-tasting water. It is, however, highly effective. Contrary to previous thinking, boiling immediately kills all diarrhea-causing microorganisms. According to Dr. Howard Backer, M.D., also a lecturer at the University of California–Berkeley, any water is adequately disinfected by the time it reaches its boiling point—even at 24,000 feet, where water boils at 135 degrees Fahrenheit.

Chemical treatment means adding halogens to water. Chlorine is the choice for municipal water supplies, and iodine has been used by the military since the beginning of the century. For backpackers, climbers, and cavers, the choice is usually Halazone (chlorine) or Aqua Potable (iodine). Both kill viruses, bacteria, and protozoa cysts, like *Giardia.* The downside: Chemical treatment, especially iodine, alters the taste of the water. Neither is recommended for babies, small children, or nursing mothers. Too much of either chemical can be fatal to humans, and babies are especially vulnerable. Iodine may enter the milk of nursing mothers. Halazone is unstable and should be replaced every couple of years.

A third option available today is filtration, which works great on most microorganisms, although some miss viruses, which are not really an issue in the waters of North America. Filter pores must be 5 microns or smaller to be effective against *Giardia.* Filters tend to be expensive ($40 to $250), but they last a long time, don't weigh much, and are usually the best solution. There are now many models from which to choose, some smaller than your water bottle. Filters can clog, so make sure the one you buy can be easily cleaned or has a replaceable filter. When treating cloudy or debris-littered water, first strain it through cheesecloth or coffee filters.

Treatment of Giardiasis. The incubation period from ingestion to the onset of infection is one to three weeks. Symptoms include malodorous stools, flatus, abdominal cramping, bloating, "sulfur burps," and indigestion. If untreated, an infection of giardiasis can last for years, accompanied by fatigue and significant weight loss. If you think you have giardiasis, you should see a doctor for a stool test. Unfortunately, the cysts don't always show up in the first stool test (three tests are recommended). Also, you can be an asymptomatic passer of cysts, and the symptoms are nonspecific—that is, they are common to other intestinal disorders. If you do have giardiasis, the treatment is five to ten days of a medicine called Flagyl. If diarrhea is a symptom, the patient should drink lots of fluids to replace those lost in feces.

A safety- and conservation-minded caver would never do the following:

- Run or jump in a cave, for even a twisted ankle could require a major rescue effort.
- Cave alone.
- Climb a rope hand over hand (as opposed to using mechanical ascenders or rappel devices).
- Use a flashlight as the primary light source. Most cavers use headlamps, along with two other backup lights.
- Break or remove formations in caves. Because cave formations can take thousands of years to develop, the NSS compares destruction of formations to killing endangered species.
- Paint arrows or graffiti on cave walls. There are better ways to mark your return route through a cave.
- Dump spent carbide in a cave or on the ground outside. Besides being unsightly, the white ash from used carbide can poison animals that eat it.
- Visit a cave without telling a responsible person exactly which cave he is exploring and the expected return time.

CARE GIVING

If someone in your party is felled by injury or illness, be prepared to take the right action. Because circumstances differ with each incident, you may have to adjust the following checklist to meet your needs.

- In the rush to aid the victim, make sure the same thing doesn't happen to someone else, such as falling down the same shaft, getting hit with continuing rockfall, being swept down the same waterway.
- Get to the victim as quickly as possible, using all necessary safety precautions.
- See that no further harm befalls the victim. If necessary, move her to a safe spot, administer first aid, reassure and comfort her, and assess the situation.
- If necessary, send two of the best cavers in the party for help. (Keep in mind, however, that self-help may be the best solution and that a rescue team should not be called in unnecessarily.) They should carry a note stating what happened to whom, where, when, and what help is needed. Include the name, address, and age of the victim. In some major caving regions, there are special telephone numbers for cave rescues.
- Continue to care for the victim. Reassurance improves morale and bolsters the will to live. Insulation combats exposure.
- If you are awaiting a rescue team, do what you can to ease its approach, such as clearing passages or fixing ropes.

CAVE DIVING

On a planet with ever-diminishing frontiers, cave diving—exploring underwater caves with scuba gear—is truly at the vanguard of adventure sports. It is also beyond the purview of this book. But the sport attracts new converts every year, many of them unprepared for what awaits them. Here, then, is a brief primer on the exotic and dangerous sport of cave diving.

It would be difficult to find a sport with higher risks than cave diving. The submerged caves of Florida, to name just one popular destination, claimed the lives of 234 divers between 1960 and 1980. It is an activity whose sum is greater than its parts. That is, you may have done a little caving and a little scuba diving, but that doesn't mean you're ready for cave diving.

The difference is that if you have a problem in open water, you can surface; in an underwater cave, you must exit both horizontally and vertically. At times, visibility can go from 200 feet to zero in seconds—or even sooner if your light fails. Underwater caves can be such labyrinths that it's hard to find your way back, even with fixed lines. And buddy breathing (sharing air) is often impossible in tight passages.

The real bugaboo for cave divers is the air they have to breathe—both its composition and pressure. For every 33 feet a diver descends, another atmosphere of pressure is added. At sea level you are at approximately one atmosphere, at 33 feet you are at two atmospheres, and so on. As a diver descends, she must constantly equalize her own internal pressure with the increasing external pressure. Sustained breathing equalizes the lungs, but the ears must be cleared through the eustachian tubes, the air ducts between the inner ear and the sinuses. Clearing can be difficult for some people, and failure to clear adequately on descent can injure the ears.

The National Speleological Society's seven ways to reduce the risk of caving:
1. Train and improve by joining an experienced group.
2. Never go caving alone; the safe minimum is three or four cavers.
3. Always carry three sources of light.
4. Don't attempt caves beyond your abilities.
5. Use proper gear, including hard hat and suitable clothing.
6. Leave word with family and friends about your location and expected return.
7. Always choose the safer alternative when you have an option.

On ascent, divers are taught to breathe constantly, so as to expel high-pressure air and avoid bursting the fragile alveoli in the lungs. This can occur in only slight depth changes if the lungs are full of air. If a diver removes or loses her regulator, she should "blow bubbles."

The deeper one goes, the higher the pressure and the more gas that is driven into solution in body fluids. Nitrogen is the most common gas, making up almost 80 percent of our air. Normally it is chemically inert and has no effect on body chemistry, but at depth it has an intoxicating effect, known as nitrogen narcosis. It has been compared to having another martini every 33 feet you descend. Assuming the diver doesn't go down too far or come up too fast, this is reversed upon rising and has no residual effect on the caver.

As the diver keeps going down, the increased pressure drives more and more nitrogen into solution in bodily fluids. If too much nitrogen is dissolved or if the diver surfaces too quickly, this nitrogen can form bubbles in the bloodstream. These bubbles tend to collect at the joints and cause pain, a disorder known as the bends or, formally, decompression sickness. This can, in severe cases, cause osteonecrosis (literally, bone death) or even diver death.

Dive tables and computers help monitor depth as a function of time and calculate nitrogen absorption. These calculations are used to establish time limits at various depths. Staying within these limits prevents the bends in most people, but anyone diving near the limits is at risk. Established limits for depths of 40, 60, 80, 100, and 120 feet are 140, 55, 30, 20, and 13 minutes, respectively.

Deep-water divers use a sophisticated system of mixed gases to reduce the impact of nitrogen at depth. These new mixtures, which replace nitrogen with oxygen or helium, carry risks of their own. Boosted oxygen content can lead to underwater seizures (the deeper a diver goes, the lower the percentage of oxygen she can tolerate), and helium demands a complete retooling of the decompression tables. This is why recreational divers are cautioned to remain above 130 feet. Technical divers who exceed that limit must pause at various depths for extended periods to blow off nitrogen.

Perhaps now you understand why technical training is essential. You must take a scuba course and get a certification card, or C card, before a shop will even fill your tank. And before you begin a cavern-diving course, you should have both basic and advanced scuba training. Some say you should not begin cavern or cave diving before you've had at least fifty dives under various open-water conditions. According to the NSS Cave Diving Section, lack of diver training is the single biggest factor in cave-diving drownings.

Even if you're an accomplished scuba diver, proper training is essential before you dive into a cave. Training programs consist of both theory and practical applications. Skills training is conducted in a swimming pool.

In the theoretical training, qualified instructors with cave-diving experience should cover the following material:

Lesson I: Review trainee qualifications and logbooks; written test on diving theory; pool test on basic diving skills

Lesson II: Cave geology and dry cave exploration techniques; basic scuba skills practiced in total darkness without mask; emphasis on sharing air

Lesson III: Cave-diving equipment; operations; organization and planning aspects; safety line technique and use of underwater lights

Lesson IV: Diving procedures and techniques; analysis of cave-diving accidents; simulated cave dive in pool using plastic tubes and obstacle courses; entanglement

Lesson V: Cave-diving areas of the United States; analysis of dive planning procedures for various caves

If you live near, or can travel to, a cave-diving locality, practical training in sinkholes and caves should follow the basic orientation lessons. You should hold a basic diver certification, pass a medical examination, and provide proof of fifty to one hundred hours of underwater diving time. Each trainee will be required to have a twin 70-cubic-foot cylinder scuba, safety line and reel, primary and emergency underwater lights, depth gauge, watch, and complete basic equipment.

The best student-instructor ratio is 1:1; however, if there is a shortage of qualified instructors, the ratio can rise to 3:1, but no higher.

Lesson I: Orientation; inspection of equipment; sinkhole diving

Lesson II: Shallow cave dive; tunnel work with no current

Lesson III: Spring dive; boil and syphon orientation

Lesson IV: Cave dive; silting; simulated rescue of diver in danger
Lesson V: Student project cave dive: deep penetration
Lesson VI: Student project cave dive: depth.

The certification levels, from beginning to advanced, are cavern, introductory cave diver, journeyman cave diver, and full cave diver. Contact the NSS-CDS for certification requirements at each level.

Besides getting the bends, other cave-diving hazards include becoming lost, separated from the boat, or entangled in fishing line, or being swept away by a current, trapped by deteriorating surf conditions, stung by a jellyfish, or eaten by a shark. If you are informed and careful, however, none of these things are likely to happen. An analysis of Florida cave-diving accidents has shown that at least one of the following admonitions was ignored in every incident:

- Reserve two-thirds of your starting air supply for the trip out of the cave. This will leave air time for you to handle emergencies. Do not begin a dive with less than 1,500 psi, and monitor your submersible pressure gauge constantly.
- Run a single, continuous guideline from the cave entrance throughout the dive. Secure the line first in open water and then inside the cave to prevent its removal by swimmers or open-water divers.
- Avoid deep diving in caves. The average depth of fatal dives in which the first two procedures were followed was more than 150 feet. Confine your cave dives to depths less than 130 feet.

Cave-Diving Accidents

Divers of the National Speleological Society have a dark saying that "anyone can die at any time on any cave dive."

In the event of a cave-diving accident, immediately notify the local sheriff's or police department and, if the suspected victim is still in the cave, ask them to contact the National Speleological Society's Cave Diving Search and Recovery Team; or the National Cave Rescue Commission, telephone: (800) 851-3051.

For the location of recompression chambers for treating decompression sickness, call (512) 536-3278 twenty-four hours a day.

Until the spring of 1994, Sheck Exley was the world's leading cave diver. Over the years, he had inched the world depth record deeper and deeper, eventually reaching 867 feet during a 1989 dive into Nacimiento Mante, a pit in northeastern Mexico. But it was Zacaton, also in Mexico, the deepest flooded cave yet discovered, that excited Exley.

On the morning of April 6, 1994, the ruggedly handsome Exley, forty-five, and Jim Bowden, fifty-two, who had first discovered Zacaton in 1989, dropped into the 87-degree water with about 200 pounds of equipment on their backs. What they were doing was pit diving, a specialized variation of cave diving in which divers free-fall for hundreds of feet in current-free shafts, a rigorous test of man and equipment. Exley and Bowden were aiming to be the first scuba divers to reach a depth of 1,000 feet.

From the Zacaton's lip, rocky cliffs fall straight down 70 feet to water level. Although cave diving isn't much of a spectator sport (once a cave diver plummets into the abyss, bubbles are the only visuals), more than fifty peasant farmers quietly gazed down upon them. Also in attendance was the divers' support team, which included Karen Hohle, Bowden's wife, and Mary Ellen Eckhoff, Exley's companion. They and others would dive into the pit and meet the men at various stages to provide company, backup tanks, and whatever else was needed.

Exley knew the risks of pit diving as well as anyone in the world. He had established the fundamentals of the sport in his 1979 text, *Basic Cave Diving: A Blueprint for Survival.* And over the years he had recovered the bodies of several dozen ill-fated cave divers in the limestone tunnels of central Florida. On previous dives, Exley himself had been stricken by bouts of a condition called high-pressure nervous syn-

continued

drome (HPNS), suffering "uncontrollable muscular twitches and multiple visions."

Survival was in the gas the divers would breathe. The compressed air commonly used in scuba diving—that is, down to about 130 feet—is roughly 80 percent nitrogen and 20 percent oxygen, the same ratio we breathe on land. Under the increased pressure of deep diving, however, breathing so much nitrogen can be hazardous to your health, bringing on nitrogen narcosis and decompression sickness. A growing number of technical divers were extending the limits by mixing a cocktail of gases in which nitrogen was replaced by oxygen or helium.

Problems were most likely on ascent. Exley and Bowden planned to descend rapidly, taking about twelve minutes to reach 1,000 feet, switching regulators to access the right tank at just the right depth. The ascent, in contrast, would be agonizingly slow and tedious. For nine hours, the two men would each follow a fixed rope to the surface, decompressing and breathing from thirteen tanks staggered along the way.

At about 9:45, Bowden slipped beneath the surface. Ten seconds later, Exley followed. Bowden dropped faster than the planned 80 feet per minute. At 200 feet he was shrouded in darkness. At 300 feet he switched regulators and began breathing an oxygen-nitrogen-helium mixture. At 550 feet he switched to what he calls his "bottom mix." At 800 feet he glanced to the right and saw Exley's light. "That's the last I saw of him," Bowden says. "At 925 feet I got worried that I didn't have enough volume and turned back."

Members of the support crew noticed Bowden's bubbles reappear sometime between twelve and eighteen minutes into the dive. But Exley's bubbles were absent. Concerned but in control, Mary Ellen Eckhoff dived down to take Exley an extra tank but couldn't find him. She descended to a ledge at 250 feet, but there was still no sign.

continued

Karen Hohle recalls what happened next: "I met Mary Ellen at about 100 feet on her way up. She was crying and her mask was messed up, and she wanted to go to the surface. I grabbed her gauge and saw she had gone to 278. I just held her—we stayed down for thirty minutes because we had to decompress. It was a very lonely time."

Three days later, while hoisting tanks, the team found Exley's body tangled in his line. One of his tanks still contained gas, and his depth gauge read 904 feet. What went wrong? One possibility is that he suffered another attack of HPNS, this time severe enough to cause convulsions that could make him lose his regulator. We may never know for sure.

For Bowden, a part-time diving instructor at the University of Texas who travels the globe nine months a year looking for deep, flooded caves, the quest for the bottom of Zacaton continues. "That was the whole purpose of our dive—to see the bottom," he says. "It would be the greatest insult to Sheck to shut down the project now."

Further Information

The NSS Cave Diving Section is the largest cave-diving organization in the United States, with members in almost every state. Section members are very active in diving springs in Florida, but many also dive mines and swamps in the northern states, do high-altitude sump diving in the West and motorized and stage diving in the South, dive sea caves in the Northeast, and conduct studies of various caves and springs. The Cave Diving Section sponsors a comprehensive cave diver and instructor-training program and is also active in the development of underwater rescue equipment. There is also a Safety and Techniques Committee within the NSS.

For more information, contact William Storage, 1 Devonshire Place, #2113, Boston, MA 02109, telephone (617) 742-2287, or 75250.1360 @compuserve.com (E-mail).

9

Ethics and Conservation

Caves can damage cavers, but far more often it is the other way around. Moreover, strained ligaments and broken bones will heal, but snap off a speleothem and it's broken forever, with thousands, maybe millions of years of geologic history wiped out in a single act of vandalism.

A virgin cave newly discovered may be so pristine and perfect that it takes your breath away. But apart from its aesthetic beauty, it is a museum of evolution, a repository of knowledge. Layers of silt and mud on cave floors can provide a historical record long since obliterated aboveground.

The first cave you enter probably won't be virgin; in fact, it's likely to be heavily traveled, possibly with palpable evidence of overuse: graffiti on the walls, beer cans on the floor, broken speleothems. What can be done?

The National Speleological Society is an organization "dedicated to the exploration, study, and conservation of caves." Many concerned members believe that "conservation" should be moved to the forefront.

On December 28, 1960, the Society's Board of Governors adopted the following policy:

"The National Speleological Society believes: that caves have unique scientific, recreational, and scenic values; that these values are endangered by both carelessness and intentional vandalism; that these values once gone, cannot be recovered; and that the responsibility for protecting caves must be assumed by those who study and enjoy them.

"Accordingly, the intention of the Society is to work for the preservation of caves with a realistic policy supported by effective programs for: the encouragement of self-discipline among cavers; education and research concerning the causes and prevention of cave damage; and special projects, including cooperation with other groups similarly dedicated to the conservation of natural areas. Specifically:

"All contents of a cave—formations, life, and loose deposits—are significant for its enjoyment and interpretation. Therefore, caving parties should leave a cave as they find it. They should provide means for the removal of waste; limit marking to a few, small, and removable signs as are needed for surveys; and, especially, exercise extreme care not to accidentally break or soil formations, disturb life forms, or unnecessarily increase the number of disfiguring paths through an area.

"Scientific collection is professional, selective, and minimal. The collection of mineral or biological material for display purposes, including previously broken or dead specimens, is never justified, as it encourages others to collect, and destroys the interest of the cave.

"The Society encourages projects such as: establishing cave preserves; opposing the sale of speleothems; supporting effective protective measures; cleaning and restoring overused caves; cooperating with private cave owners by providing knowledge about their cave and assisting them in protecting their cave and property from damage during cave visits; and encouraging commercial cave owners to make use of their opportunity to aid the public in understanding caves and the importance of their conservation.

"Where there is reason to believe that publication of cave locations will lead to vandalism before adequate protection can be established, the Society will oppose such publication.

"It is the duty of every Society member to take personal responsibility for spreading a consciousness of cave conservation to each potential user of caves. Without this, the beauty and value of our caves will not long remain with us."

CAVE OWNER RELATIONS

Most cave trips start with a series of questions: "Where should we go today?" "Should we go wet or dry?" "Vertical or horizontal?" "Will the owner let us into the cave?" The last question is particularly important, because all the skills and techniques in the world won't do you any good if the cave owner won't give you permission. You will improve your chances of gaining access to the cave of your choice if you act in an ethical manner.

All caves are controlled by someone, either a private landowner or a state or federal government. The procedure for gaining access is the same regardless—you ask permission. Sometimes direct contact the day of the trip is all that is needed. On the other hand, many government agencies require an advance written request and then a face-to-face interview on the day of the trip. Some private owners also prefer advance notice, especially if the group is large.

To find the owner, canvass the local grotto. Ask fellow cavers about the status of the cave. Most owners live at the cave property, and absentee owners usually have a neighbor acting as caretaker. Always have alternative caves so that your trip won't be ruined if you don't find the owner or can't get permission.

When you do find the owner, you must convince him of the following:

- You will take care of his property, including the cave.
- You will not be injured or killed in the cave.
- He will have to assume *no* responsibility for your health and safety.

It is indeed a challenge to do this in just a few minutes. It's so easy for the owner to say no, especially if he's had trouble with previous visitors. But if you are courteous and sensitive, most cave owners will let you explore their caves. They often are proud of the attention the cave receives and may even be cavers themselves. After you receive permission, it is then your ethical duty to act properly and not ruin the chances of the next caving party.

No matter what you do or say, some owners will always say no, some will always say yes, and the rest will be on the fence. Persuading someone to agree to what you want demands basic people skills. When approaching a landowner, consider the following suggestions:

- Choose a reasonable time to approach, especially if you don't know the landowner. Avoid Sunday mornings and after sunset.
- Send one person, your most personable and able communicator, to make the initial greeting. A mob can be intimidating. Knock on the door and step back. If the owner won't open the door to a stranger, an increasingly common occurrence, try to sound friendly and unthreatening as you speak through the door. If you find him outside, approach calling "Hello!" before getting too close.
- Introduce yourself and state your business, speaking slowly and clearly. The words should sound spontaneous, but you might say something like this: "Hello, my name is Peter Smith. I'm interested in a cave over there (indicate the direction). I understand the cave is on your property."
- Listen to the owner's response and gauge his attitude. If he is friendly, ask about the cave: "I understand it's pretty (or has speleothems)." If you sense that his attitude is favorable, it might be time to ask, "I was wondering if it would be all right to go into the cave." If he is not so friendly, you need to start building his confidence in you.
- The key to boosting the owner's confidence in you may lie in the small points. The undecided cave owner will scrutinize you, trying to decide whether you're responsible, careful, considerate—all the things he has a right to expect. He can only go on what he sees and hears. Avoid the little things that may trigger a negative response, such as sunglasses or a low-slung hat. Dress in clean, respectable clothes and comb your hair. A pack of cigarettes in your pocket may mean nothing to you or your friends, but it may be a turn-off to a nonsmoker. Alcohol, which connotes careless behavior to some, should be neither

displayed nor consumed on the owner's property. Speak kindly to the dog, wife, and children. In fact, address the wife as though she has just as much say as the husband; she may have more. Don't mumble, look at the ground, or scuffle your feet. Make good eye contact, smile, and speak clearly. Appear humble yet confident.

- Say thank you. All we really have to give cave owners—and all most of them want—is full cooperation and appreciation. After your trip, you can show your gratitude by dropping by and thanking the owner. Offer to send him pictures of the cave—and be sure to send them! At least one cave has been closed because a caver forgot his promise. Some grottos and cavers send Christmas cards to cave owners.

- If the owner is firm in his rejection, accept it graciously. If you remain polite, you may succeed another day. If the owner says no but is reasonably friendly and keeps chatting, you may gently probe for his concerns. His reason may be a desire for privacy, knee-jerk possessiveness about his property, fear of legal liability or damage to the cave, anger at previous cavers who didn't play by the rules, or a combination of all of the above. Still, more than one friendly, silver-tongued caver has deflected those concerns and converted a no into a yes.

If the cave is on government land, the same people skills still apply. Public land does not mean you are automatically entitled to visit the cave. Some caves on public land don't require permission, some do, and others are permanently closed. Do your research. Government managers are entrusted to do the same thing that private owners do—protect the property and ensure that the people entering caves can do so safely. They will probably ask the same questions, and you need to answer them.

Whether you're dealing with a private landowner or a government bureaucrat, treat him with respect and courtesy. In other words, more honey, less vinegar. We ignore good owner relations at our peril. More than one irate cave owner has dynamited or gated a cave entrance.

For more information, contact the NSS Land Owner Relations Committee, c/o Bill Thoman, 4905 Ralph Ave., Cincinnati, OH 45238; (513) 251-7357.

COLLECTING CAVE LIFE

The enduring rule of the NSS regarding collection of cave life is usually translated thus: "Do not collect cave life except under specific direction of a scientist." Although such a strict prohibition is a useful warning for novices, it needs elaboration for experienced cavers with an active interest in the science of caves.

Although the NSS continues to discourage unnecessary disturbance of cave life, especially if there is no scientific or conservationist value, cavers all over the country have helped biospeleologists by making small, strategic collections of cave animals. For example, members of the Texas Speleological Society have contributed greatly to the body of knowledge available on cave fauna of Texas and Mexico. They have routinely made controlled collections in little-traveled caves and sent them to scientists. This is, at the very least, a loose interpretation of "specific direction."

Even the staunchest conservationist should agree that we cannot protect cave life unless we have detailed knowledge of what is living in caves. We must have published scientific information on cave fauna before we can know what to protect and before we can pursue legal action, such as qualifying species as either threatened or endangered.

Another fact arguing for limited, controlled fauna collection is that cave animals, unlike speleothems, do reproduce. Many cave populations are neither fragile nor endangered.

Although no general rule is applicable in all situations, we may start with the basic precept, as expressed by William R. Elliott, former chairman of the Texas Speleological Society, that "the amateur collectors should not collect in caves that have been well-studied or are ecologically damaged, unless at the specific request of a scientist who knows the situation and asks for specific numbers of a certain species. If the caver is in serious doubt about the conditions, he should not collect, but he should make observations and notes. No collections should be made unless the caver already knows a scientist who will take the collections and put them to good use."

In some caves, a stricter prohibition is necessary. Just visiting certain bat caves can be harmful, especially if the animals are hibernating in the winter or giving birth in the spring. Disturbing hibernating bats can cause them to deplete their fat reserves and die. Consequently, bat biologists and cavers have designated certain caves as off-limits, at least for part of the year. The key is knowing the region and its limitations. Work with the local grotto and take advantage of its store of collective knowledge.

How to Collect

If you do have the okay to make cave collections, a simple collecting kit is a 1- or 2-ounce screw-cap jar containing 70 to 80 percent ethyl or isopropyl (rubbing) alcohol. Isopropyl is cheap and can be found in most drug and grocery stores. Baby-food jars work well if they have screw-on lids; avoid snap-on lids.

Most animals can be preserved in alcohol, but formaldehyde is best for fish, frogs, earthworms, and salamanders. Drugstore formaldehyde is usually 40 percent and should be diluted, ten parts water to one part formaldehyde. Plastic baby bottles are good containers for formaldehyde, especially if you tape the lid shut.

Carry plenty of jars, using a different one in each of the cave's habitats: entrance area, pond, guano deposit, and so on. To avoid smaller species being damaged by larger ones, such as large spiders, millipedes, beetles, and crickets, put them in separate jars.

Collecting tools are not always necessary, and some are downright harmful. Most tweezers and forceps are too stiff and run the risk of crushing the specimen. Arthropods can usually be picked up with your fingers. To catch crickets, you need quick hands and a delicate touch. After trapping one under your cupped hand, gently brush it into a jar. To gather very small insects, wet your finger with alcohol, gently touch the animal, and then stick your finger back into the alcohol to dislodge it. Gently scrape ceiling creatures into a jar. Aquatic flatworms (planarians) should be taken alive and immediately air-mailed to a specialist in an insulated container having original cave

Dr. William R. Elliott, who has chaired the biology session at annual NSS conventions, makes light, flimsy forceps by using scissors to cut them out of a flattened aluminum can, in paper-doll fashion. You may have to rebend them to align the tips. They will work on all but the very largest and very smallest of specimens.

water. Carry a small aquarium dip net for most aquatic collections. To prevent tearing the netting, wrap it in a plastic bag and stash it in your pack or pocket. Tea strainers also make good nets.

Be careful not to crush the specimen or damage its antennae, legs, or tail. Often it is these appendages that enable the scientist to complete identification. A dozen or so specimens of the smaller species and two or three of the larger ones are usually sufficient for identification. Greater quantities should be collected only when requested by a qualified biologist.

Where to Look
When looking for specimens, investigate all areas of a cave. Too often the entrance area is ignored, but it too contains species of interest to biospeleologists.

Record Keeping
Many a valuable collection has been ruined by poor record keeping. A collection with inadequate or illegible data may have no scientific value and may have to be discarded. As soon after collection as possible, you should add a small collection label to each jar. The label should be in pencil or nonfading ink on strong paper, and should include the following information:

1. Name and specific location of the cave. Besides county and state, include specific information, such as topographic map coordinates, direction and distance from prominent landmarks, and cave survey number.

2. Date of collection. Spell out the month or use a Roman numeral.
3. Collector's name.
4. Description of the habitat, including temperature, if known.

THE HAPPY STORY OF HORSE CAVE

Horse Cave, in Kentucky, lies in the heart of karst land, a geologic province once located beneath the sea and now underlaid by limestone. The Swiss-cheese karst permits rainwater to leak underground nearly as fast as it falls.

The inviting entrance to Horse Cave began attracting visitors as early as 1794, and a town of twenty-eight hundred inhabitants eventually sprang up there. In 1867 John Muir stopped by on his thousand-mile walk and raved about this "noble gateway to the birthplace of springs and fountains."

In 1916 the cave was illuminated by electric lights and opened to tours. It was soon descended upon by a burgeoning automobile culture that threatened to love the cave to death. Within thirty years the town's tour business was dead, and its economy was crippled. Although some damage was done by visitors, the killing force was provided by the villagers themselves. Sewage and industrial waste dumped into the water supply found its way into the cave, killing off the blind subterranean fish and the arthropods. This created a stinky gas that wafted back up to the surface, permeating Main Street and driving visitors to seek more aromatic attractions.

The cave had been biologically dead of poisoning for decades when the resurrection began. In 1989, with pressure from the Environmental Protection Agency, the new Horse Cave sewage plant began operation. It wasn't long before sci-
continued

entists began seeing changes. Julian Lewis, a cave ecologist from the University of Louisville, had been studying the cave for years. In 1990, where once he had waded in frothing sewage, he came upon clear water and cave isopods. On a return visit in 1993, a blind cavefish—absent from Horse Cave for fifty years—swam up to his boot.

Horse Cave, now renamed Hidden River Cave, has been called the greatest cave success story in the United States. But it's a never-ending tale. Hidden River Cave, like so many other caves, is one sewage dump or chemical spill away from annihilation.

Of course, as we now know, man's destruction of Horse Cave was hardly unusual. According to Lewis, "The effects of urbanization are wiping out populations of cave animals at what's become a startling rate." Single pulses of industrial pollution have obliterated entire underground communities. Highways and housing tracts have torn up caves, in some cases wiping out the only known species of certain troglobites. "It's the same sort of mechanism as what's going on in the rain forests," says Lewis. "They're being destroyed before being discovered."

One reason for man's inhumanity to caves is a misperception that they are otherworldly, somehow disconnected from our life topside. But the interconnectedness of life extends to the earth's nether regions, and what we do on the surface has enormous consequences for caves.

Even the longest, and arguably most famous, cave system in the world, Mammoth Cave in Kentucky, has not been spared. Its 350 or so miles of explored passageways enjoy national park status, yet each year streams carrying thousands of tons of eroded soil, manure, and pesticides flow through Mammoth Cave. A dam backs up water 16 miles into the

continued

park, an assault on the only known habitats of the threatened blindfish and the endangered Kentucky cave shrimp. A gate covering one entrance has stifled ventilation and overheated the winter roost of the Indiana bat, whose population in the cave has declined precipitously in the past fifty years. And in the Snowball Dining Room, 265 feet below the earth's surface, the walls have grown dingy with dirt and fungus, the unnatural by-products of six hundred thousand annual visitors.

"Lights, lunchrooms, pavement, body heat—all of that is completely foreign to the natural cave environment," says Mike Adams, Mammoth Cave's head of interpretation. "The cave does not recover like a surface environment does. We have found prehistoric footprints four thousand years old."

NEW CAVES

Discovering a virgin cave, or even a new wing of a known cave, is a caver's dream, the thrill of a lifetime. But it also carries certain responsibilities to preserve what you've found. Try to disturb nothing: cave life, formations, even bits of wood and stone. Avoid sections of a cave that can be entered only by destroying speleothems. Take care in selecting your route—others will likely follow in your footsteps. Choose the route that will damage the cave the least.

Be an explorer, not a collector. Think of yourself as the curator of a natural museum. Accordingly, if you find something of special interest, leave it in place and alert a local scientist.

Don't remove formations; don't even touch them unnecessarily. If you subscribe to the philosophy that "no one will miss just one stalactite," consider the logical result of everyone taking that position.

When caving as a team, tread carefully and on the same track as the others. Take photos, leave only faint footprints, and kill only time.

VETERANS' RESPONSIBILITY TO ROOKIES

Unless you are a bat or a cave cricket, you were not born with caving skills. It's a talent that has to be learned, either from someone else or by trial and error. But trial and error, as the expression implies, means making mistakes, and caves are notoriously intolerant of mistakes. It's better to learn from experienced cavers. Veteran cavers have a moral obligation to instruct novices in the areas of safety, conservation, equipment, and technique.

Safety

A primary responsibility of experienced cavers is to teach new cavers about caving hazards and how to avoid them. One such hazard, for example, is loss of light. Every year novices have to be rescued from

---

CAVING ETIQUETTE

- Avoid touching or walking on any cave formations. If you destroy a speleothem, it's gone forever.
- Stay on established trails; respect closed areas.
- Do not mark the walls of the cave; defacing cave walls is strictly prohibited. Mark your route with temporary flagging and remove it on your way out.
- Do not use the rope or gear of others who may be visiting the cave at the same time.
- If a passage is too fragile, turn back.
- Take nothing but pictures. Collecting specimens or removing any materials from caves is prohibited, with the exceptions outlined in this chapter.
- Pack out what you brought in, including used carbide, trash, and human waste. Take out all your food scraps so that animals don't associate food with human presence. Pick up after others.

caves because they took only one light source—a flashlight—and it failed. The solution—carrying backup light sources—is simple enough, once you know it. Other hazards include hypothermia, exhaustion, falling rock, getting lost, and drowning. The risks of caving can be lessened by knowing these hazards exist and taking the appropriate measures to prevent them.

Start to build a newcomer's confidence by addressing and allaying his fears. No, the cave won't collapse on you. No, bats will not suck your blood. Begin by exploring caves well within the beginner's skill range. Limit the trip to a reasonable length. Travel at a speed comfortable for the slowest member of your group. Slow down and help the stragglers. Even on moderate terrain, belay new cavers. Watch them closely for signs of hypothermia, dehydration, exhaustion, claustrophobia, or injury. Newcomers may not recognize the warning signs, or they may be reluctant to admit they're having trouble. If a serious problem does arise, don't hesitate to abort the trip. You can return later.

Not all experienced cavers should be teachers. You can be an accomplished caver and still be a poor communicator. At the very least, though, you can be a good example.

Teaching new cavers is very worthwhile. Newcomers are going to go caving whether they get help or not. By ensuring that those entering the sport are safety-minded, conscientious, qualified cavers, you help ensure that caves will remain open to future cavers. If we lose the caves, we lose caving.

Conservation

Ignorance is also at the root of most cave damage. Novices must be taught to be caretakers of caves. The veteran caver should instill protection ethics in the novice. Instead of simply handing the beginner a list of do's and don'ts, help him interpret caves, explaining how they were formed, what unique life forms live underground, how fragile caves are, and how human intrusion adversely affects them. From knowledge springs respect.

Above all, experienced cavers should be role models for the art of soft caving. They should constantly demonstrate good, conscientious techniques, striving in their actions as well as their words to make every newcomer a passionate defender of caves and cave biota. Ideally, then, newcomers will go on to monitor not only their own behavior but that of their partners, too. Peer pressure is a powerful tool.

Equipment and Technique

The veteran also should offer advice and instruction regarding equipment and technique. When new cavers have their own gear, inspect it to make sure it is adequate and in good shape. This may involve repairing or lending equipment. It is mandatory that each caver have a helmet, a good headlamp, at least two independent backup lights, and adequate clothing and boots. Explain the need for durable garb that can withstand rough, dirty conditions. Gloves, knee and elbow pads, and a small pack are usually musts. Warn new climbers that mud and abrasion will quickly trash a zippered pack.

Also make sure that newcomers know how to use their equipment. Most cavers recommend that beginners start with a simple electric light system. Carbide lamps can be heavy and temperamental and can suck the fun right out of the first caving experience. Moreover, the brighter electric light will let the beginner see farther, making it easier to remember the details necessary to find his way into and out of the cave. After rookies become accustomed to the sport, they can be introduced to carbide for its unique advantages.

Teach beginning cavers as many techniques as possible before you go underground. Encourage them to attend instructional seminars at the local grotto. Once underground, set a good example and keep an eye on the less-experienced members of your party, offering guidance as needed. Keep in mind that people tend to get defensive about their accomplishments, even when they are starting out, so mix in plenty of praise and encouragement to soften the criticism.

PROJECT CAVING

We have an impact on every cave we enter. No matter how softly we tread, we leave a mark here, a smudge there. Some cavers, believing it is selfish and unethical to continue to take and take from caves without giving something back, have undertaken what is called project caving.

Project caving is the coming together of a group of people to achieve a specific goal in a cave or cave system. It may involve surveys, hydrology, or restoration and may take months or even years to complete. The data collected are then used to understand and protect the cave.

Although the focus is to *give*, volunteers can also figure to *get* a lot from project caving. Some of the rewards are as follows:

- You make new friends. Project cavers work together closely, and you are bound to make contacts for future cave trips or projects.
- You improve your caving skills. The people working on projects tend to be accomplished cavers, and you can learn from

Project caving; a cave campsite in Belize

them. Many will be willing to take time out to help you advance your skills.

- You gain knowledge. As you work on a project, you learn about cave geology, hydrology, and other sciences. If you survey, you will become intimate with the section of the cave you work in. You will naturally tune in to your surroundings.
- You will gain the respect of your peers. We tend to respect those who demonstrate long-term dedication to a worthwhile project.
- You will have fun.

Choose a project that is compatible with your skills. If you get in over your head or are ill prepared, the other cavers will resent having to baby-sit you. Contact the head of the project and find out how you can contribute. Then go prepared to have fun and give something back to a cave.

CONSERVATION EFFORTS

To learn more and educate others, many cavers have come together in study groups, conservation task forces, and regional and state cave surveys. By getting involved in one or more of these efforts, you and your group can make a real contribution to cave preservation. Consider doing one or more of the following:

- Become students of caves. Get beyond admiration into research. Read scientific journals and bulletins.
- Attend public hearings held by government agencies on land-use policies.
- Petition government agencies and politicians to rectify caving injustices.
- Generate publicity for key and critical causes by communicating with the media, perhaps by writing articles or letters.
- Buy land and caves for nature preserves, or lend support to agencies, such as the National Speleology Society and the Nature Conservancy, that do just that.

Although the vast majority of cavers are passive conservationists—that is, they conserve by *not* doing bad things—every year more and more caves fall victim to pollution, trash dumping, land devel-

The Nature Conservancy has done a lot to protect caves. At least 113 Conservancy preserves in the United States are centered around caves, many of them in the Appalachians. One is Hubbard's Cave in Tennessee, ranked as one of the three most important bat-hibernation sites in the country. Each winter, eight species of bats from six states descend on Hubbard's, including some 250,000 gray bats, a huge share of an endangered species whose numbers have been plummeting, partly due to club-wielding bat haters who had been creeping into the cave and killing the animals in their sleep.

The Nature Conservancy bought the cave and fifty acres surrounding it. Working with teams of cavers, engineers, and the National Guard, they installed one of the largest bat-cave gates ever, a 30-ton grate of steel more than 30 feet tall and 35 feet wide. It not only keeps the vandals out, but it also allows the cave to "breathe" and the bats to enter and exit.

opment, quarrying, and dam building. It's a classic case of tyranny of an uncaring minority, and the resulting loss of habitat and food resources can be extremely destructive of cave ecology. Caves are unique treasures deserving your respect and tender care. Do more than your share to protect them.

GLOSSARY

aa: solidified lava with a rough texture. Composed of chunky fragments melted together. Usually lacks lava tubes. (Contrasted with *pahoehoe.*)

active: said of a cave or cave passage with water running through it, or with speleothems still growing from fresh deposition.

aerobic exercise: a continuous, rhythmic exercise during which the body's oxygen needs are still being met. Aerobic activities, which condition the body to burn fat, include brisk walking, running, swimming, cycling, and cross-country skiing. A conditioned athlete can carry on aerobic exercise for a long time. (Contrasted with *anaerobic exercise.*)

aid climbing: the technique of moving up a rock face resting on artificial holds. Slings, ropes, nuts, and other paraphernalia are used for physical support, not just for emergency protection or belay anchors. (Contrasted with *free climbing.*)

anaerobic exercise: exercise at an intensity level that exceeds the ability of the body to dispose of the lactic acid produced by the muscles. As a result, this exercise, which uses glycogen (stored sugars) as its main fuel, can be sustained for only a short time before exhaustion sets in. Examples of anaerobic exercise include weight lifting, sprinting, and vigorous calisthenics. (Contrast with *aerobic exercise.*)

anchor: the point at which a fixed rope, a rappel rope, or a belay is secured to rock, snow, or ice by any of various means.

aragonite: fairly rare crystalline form of calcium carbonate found in caves (the more common is calcite), usually as needlelike formations.

ascend: to climb a fixed rope with the aid of mechanical ascenders.

ascender: a mechanical device, such as a Jumar, Gibbs, or Shunt, that works on a ratchet principle. The device will slide up a rope but will grip securely when it gets a downward pull, thus permitting climbers to move up a rope and not slide down. Ascender knots (see *prusik*) serve the same purpose.

ballistic stretching: quick, bouncing stretches that force muscles to lengthen. The muscles react by reflexively contracting or shortening, increasing the likelihood of muscle tears and soreness.

bandolier: a chest loop for carrying climbing equipment.

bed: a layer of rock.

bedding plane: the contact point between two dissimilar beds. These may part and form a thin crack or one several inches wide. Cave passages often form preferentially along these inherently weaker lines, such as where limestone and shale meet.

belay: to tend the climbing rope by maintaining an appropriate degree of slack or tension, ready to immediately put enough friction on the rope to hold the caver in case of a fall. Friction is generated by the rope passing around the belayer's body or through a belay device. Belaying is the primary safeguard in climbing, and its practice is universal. *Belay* also refers to the entire system set up to make belaying possible, including the anchor that holds the belayer in place.

belay device: any of numerous small metal gadgets that force a bend in the climbing rope, creating enough friction to enable a belayer to hold a fall. See also *descender* and *figure-eight descender.*

bight: a loop of rope.

biner (pronounced "beaner"): slang for *carabiner.*

bivouac: a night out without a tent.

bivouac sack: a lightweight, unfilled, waterproof nylon bag that can cover a sleeping bag or a climber caught without a sleeping bag. Also called *bivy sack.*

bivy: slang for *bivouac.*

blowing cave: a cave that has large air currents moving in and out for extended periods, in response to changes in barometric pressure.

bobbin: a rappel device favored by many cavers.

body belay: see *waist belay.*

bombproof: said of a hold or belay that will not fail, regardless of how much weight or force is put on it.

boneyard: a type of passage formation, prevalent in the Guadalupe Mountains of New Mexico, that is a seemingly random network of interconnected tubes rather than a single, large conduit. Formed below the water table.

bowline: knot used to make a nonslipping loop in the end of the rope.

boxwork: honeycomblike speleothem projecting from a cave wall or ceiling; results from exposure of veins of more resistant (less soluble) materials that have filled cracks in the rock.

brake bar: a small aluminum rod about 3/4 by 2 1/2 inches that is placed on a rappel rack or on an arrangement of carabiners to create friction on the rope for rappelling.

breakdown: rock slabs, blocks, or chips on a cave floor that have fallen from the walls or ceiling, usually when a cave drains, removing the buoyancy offered by water.

bridging: a climbing technique in which the climber pushes out to the sides with hands and/or feet, using opposing pressure against the rock. Often used in climbing *chimneys* or *dihedrals.* Also called *stemming.*

cable ladder: a lightweight ladder made of two parallel, stainless-steel cables with metal rungs held in place by metal ferrules crimped to the cables.

cairn: a small pile of stones used to mark a trail, route, passage junction, or some other feature.

calcite: the common crystalline form of calcium carbonate, $CaCO_3$, formed by the deposition of dissolved limestone. It is the main mineral in most limestone speleothems and is the most common cave mineral.

carabiner: an oval or D-shaped metal snap-link about 3 inches long in the shape of a giant safety pin. Capable of holding a ton or more, carabiners are used for many chores, including attaching the rope to anchors. See *locking carabiner.*

carabiner brake: a configuration of four to six carabiners arranged to provide rope friction for rappelling.

carbide lamp: a lamp that produces light by burning acetylene gas resulting from a mix of carbide and water. Carbide is short for the rocklike chemical calcium carbide, CaC_2.

carbon dioxide: the gas that, dissolved in water, forms carbonic acid. Excess CO_2 in caves lacking air flow can be a hazard.

carbonic acid: a weak acid made from carbon dioxide and rain or soil water. It is responsible for the corrosion of limestone and hence the formation of most caves.

cave: a naturally formed void in the earth that does not necessarily have an opening to the surface.

cave pearl: a small, round calcite formation deposited in a shallow cave pool or floor depression.

caver: a person who explores caves in a safe, respectful manner. A true caver shows respect for the environment, other cavers, and the cave owner.

cavern: a large cave. It is often used to describe show caves.

cave system: a series of caves that are, or once were, connected.

chert: a hard, usually black mineral composed of silica, often found in the cracks and fissures of limestone.

chest harness: a harness used in conjunction with a waist harness to attach a caver to the rope.

chimney: a vertical or near-vertical shaft or fissure, either tubular or where two walls come close together, that is wide enough to accommodate a caver's entire body.

chimney effect: a seasonal phenomenon associated with multiple-entrance caves in which cold air flows out the bottom while warmer air is sucked in above (summer) or vice versa (winter).

chimneying: the method of climbing a chimney using the pressure of feet and back on opposing walls.

chockstone: a rock wedged in a crack or behind a flake, around which a runner can be threaded and then clipped to a rope for an anchor point. Before artificial chocks, British climbers used to carry pebbles to place in cracks; later they used hexagonal machine nuts found on railroad tracks. Today there are two basic types of chocks: wedges and hexes. See also *nut*.

clean climbing: means of ascent and descent that leave the rock unscarred and undamaged after the caving team has passed.

climbing calls: signals, usually verbal, used between cavers while climbing, such as "Belay is on" and "Ready to climb."

clip in: to attach oneself to an anchor or rope, usually with a carabiner.

Clog: a British company that manufactures climbing hardware.

coiling: the various methods of looping and tying a rope so that it can be carried, requiring a certain amount of skill to avoid kinking.

column: a speleothem created when a stalactite meets a stalagmite.

commercial cave: see *show cave*.

contour interval: on a topographic map, the difference in elevation between one contour line and the one next to it.

contour line: a line on a topographic map, any point of which is the same elevation above sea level. The line indicating the boundary of a lake could be on a contour line.

corkscrew passage: a twisting passage, often a tight crawlway or fissure.

crack: a gap or fracture in the rock, varying in width from a thin seam to a wide chimney.

crawlway: a cave passage small enough to force a caver to move on his hands and knees or to crawl on his belly or back.

crevice: a narrow opening or fissure in the floor of a cave.

dark zone: the areas of a cave far enough from an entrance that sunlight never penetrates. The true cave environment, it is an unusually stable region. With little wind, a relative humidity near 100 percent, and a relatively constant temperature, the dark zone is as silent and dark as a tomb. The environment could hardly seem less hospitable to life, yet, astonishingly, some species thrive in the deep recesses of the earth, albeit with physical adaptations.

daypack: a medium-sized soft pack, favored by cavers for carrying food, water, and other supplies; bigger than a fanny pack, smaller than a backpack.

dead cave: a cave in which speleothems have stopped growing because water is no longer seeping into the cave.

dehydration: a depletion of body fluids that can hinder the body's ability to regulate its own temperature. One can become dehydrated during caving activities if the fluids lost from perspiration and respiration are not replaced by drinking water. Chronic dehydration lowers a caver's tolerance to fatigue, reduces his ability to sweat, elevates his rectal temperature, and increases the stress on his circulatory system. In general, a loss of 2 percent or more of one's body weight by sweating affects performance; a loss of 5 to 6 percent affects health.

descender: a friction device used for descending ropes (rappelling). The most common are the *rappel rack, figure-eight,* and *bobbin;* others include the *brake bar* and the *carabiner brake.* Also known as a *rappel device.*

diaper sling: a rigged harness for rappelling, usually made of 1-inch nylon webbing.

dig: to try to break into a cave or a new area of a known cave by excavation or by blasting.

double brake bar: a rappel device consisting of two carabiners with a brake bar on each one and connected by a third carabiner or metal ring.

drapery: a thin curtain-shaped speleothem caused by a sheet of running water flowing down a wall rather than by a series of free-falling drops in one place.

dripstone: any of several calcite deposits, including stalactites, stalagmites, and flowstone, caused by deposition from dripping, calcite-saturated water.

drop: a descending slope, pit, or pitch, usually requiring a rope.

duck: British term for a cave passage in which the water is nearly to the roof.

Dulfursitz rappel: antiquated method of descending in which a caver threads an anchored climbing rope between his legs, returns it to the front of his body, then wraps it over a shoulder and holds it behind him with one hand.

edging: using the sides of one's boots to stand on thin rock ledges.

electric lamp: an arrangement of bulb, reflector, and lens generally mounted on a caver's helmet, often with a wire running to a battery worn elsewhere on the body.

endurance: the ability to withstand pain, stress, or fatigue and keep going.

entrainment: low-level air movement through a cave caused by flowing water dragging air along above its surface.

entrance zone: the area of a cave near its entrance. The entrance zone has most of the same environmental conditions as the surface. Animals have long sought refuge in entrance zones, and humans have used them for shelter and burial grounds since prehistoric times.

etrier: a short, foldable ladder of three to five steps with a small loop at the top for attaching to an aid point. Usually made from webbing sewn or knotted to form loops for the feet, it is used by cavers primarily to negotiate difficult lips.

expansion bolt: a type of anchor that expands and locks when screwed into a prebored hole in the limestone. Used when a rock lacks cracks into which a piton or nut can be inserted. Bolts provide the safest protection, but they permanently alter the rock.

face: a wall of rock steeper than 60 degrees.

face climbing: using handholds and footholds on an open rock face.

face holds: edges and irregularities protruding from a wall, or the pockets sunk into it.

false floor: a thin floor made of calcite or lava under which dirt or gravel has eroded or worked away.

fanny pack: a small, soft pack worn around the waist for holding a few emergency supplies.

figure-eight descender: a metal rappelling device in the shape of the numeral 8. One hole is used to attach the device to a harness with a carabiner. A rope is passed through the other hole to provide friction for the descent.

figure-eight knot: a versatile knot with several forms; the recommended knot for tying a loop in the middle of a rope and for attaching rappel ropes to their anchors.

fissure: a narrow crack, break, or fracture. Fissures and crevices are usually negotiated by chimneying or traversing.

fitness: ability to put one's health to work in a dynamic way. One can be healthy without being fit, but not the reverse.

fixed protection: anchors, such as bolts or pitons, that are permanently placed in the rock.

fixed rope: a rope anchored and left in place so that cavers can ascend and descend at will.

flagging tape: thin plastic ribbon of various colors used for marking passages, survey stations, or trails.

flexibility: the ability of the joints to move through their full range of motion. Good flexibility protects muscles and ligaments from pulls and tears.

flowstone: calcite deposits that have accumulated from water slowly flowing along a cave floor or wall.

formation: a mineral deposit with distinctive characteristics, such as a stalactite, whether formed from calcite or more exotic minerals. See *speleothem.*

free climbing: climbing in which natural handholds and footholds are used. Hardware is used only for protection and not for support or progress. (Contrasted with *aid climbing.*)

friction brake: a device that provides rope friction when rappeling, such as a bar mounted on one or more carabiners.

Friend: an active (spring-loaded) camming device inserted into a crack as an anchor point. Designed and marketed by Ray Jardine in 1978, the Friend was a major breakthrough because it allowed cavers and climbers to protect roofs and parallel cracks with minimal damage and minimal time spent making the placement.

Gibbs: a cam-type mechanical ascending device invented by a caver, Charlie Gibbs, and favored by many cavers.

Gore-Tex: a material used for clothing and tents that allows water vapor from the body to escape but will not allow liquid water droplets (rain) to enter. It has high breathability.

gorp: a high-carbohydrate snack food made primarily from nuts and dried fruit; an acronym for "good ol' raisins and peanuts."

groove: a shallow, vertical crack.

grotto: a caving club or chapter under the umbrella of the National Speleological Society. Members of a grotto usually reside in the same general area. Also, a small cave or chamber.

guano: the droppings of bats that collect on the floors of some caves.

Guano can be a critical link in the chain of cave life.

gypsum: a common cave mineral composed of hydrous calcium sulfate, $CaSO_4$. $2H_2O$, usually deposited under drier conditions than calcite.

gypsum flowers: delicate speleothems, often of great beauty, in which gypsum grows long, twisting crystals. Also called *oulophites.*

hand line: a short (10–30 feet) fixed rope used for climbing or scrambling on steep pitches or narrow ledges, when holds are scarce.

hanging belay: a belay station on vertical rock that offers no ledge for support.

harness: a contraption worn around the shoulders or waist, usually made of wide tape, and offering convenient loops through which to clip a rope and other gear. If a caver falls while roped onto a harness, the shock load is distributed over a wide area. The caver also has a better chance of remaining in an upright position, lowering the risk of head meeting rock.

haul bag: a bag used for holding and hauling gear up and down.

headlamp: a light that is mounted on a caver's helmet or headband.

helectite: a stalactite that instead of hanging vertically has various twists and curves. It forms from water under hydrostatic pressure.

hip belay: see *waist belay.*

hold: a protrusion or indentation in the rock that a caver can grasp with fingers (handhold) or stand on (foothold).

hydrology: scientific study of underground and surface water.

hypothermia: a dangerous condition in which the body can no longer generate enough heat to compensate for heat loss. Cavers are most susceptible to hypothermia when they are wet, injured, or not moving around enough to stay warm. It can happen in minutes or take hours and can be fatal.

insurgence: a cave entrance with water entering. Also known as a *sinking stream.*

isopod: an order of crustaceans, sometimes found in caves, having a flat, oval body and seven pairs of legs.

Jumar: a trade name for a Swiss rope-gripping ascender favored by climbers.

junction: a place where two or more passages come together.

karst: terrain whose topography is formed by the dissolution of rock, usually limestone or gypsum, and characterized by solutional surface features, subterranean drainage, and caves.

kernmantle: a type of rope construction consisting of a core (kern) of braided fibers protected by an outer braided sheath (mantle).

ladder: in caving, a contraption made of aircraft cable and aluminum rungs, used for climbing out of 10- to 30-foot pits. Deeper pits are usually negotiated with an ascending device.

latitude: imaginary lines that run parallel to the equator and measure, in degrees, the distance north and south from the equator.

lava tube: a cave formed by the hardening of the outer layer of a flowing stream of molten lava, similar to a skin of ice on a frozen river.

laybacking: Grabbing a vertical edge, often a flake of rock, then pulling with hands, pushing with feet, and walking the feet up almost alongside the hands. It is a strenuous but useful technique for arêtes, corners with cracks, and cracks offset in walls. Also called *liebacking*.

lead, or leader: the first caver in a party; the head of an expedition.

leader fall: a fall taken by the lead caver. The leader will fall double the distance to the closest protection.

legend: explanatory list of the symbols and colors on a map.

ligaments: tough bands of elastic tissue that join bones together to prevent excessive movement. See *sprain.*

limestone: a gray-blue sedimentary rock deposited in sea basins and composed of calcium carbonate, $CaCO_3$. Most caves are formed by acidic water dissolving limestone.

live cave: a cave in which speleothems are still being developed by water seeping into the cave.

locking carabiner: a carabiner that can be "locked" with a barrel on a screw thread. Less common than snap-links, locking carabiners are used when there is a risk of the gate opening. Also called a *screwgate.*

maillon: a small, lightweight French version of the carabiner. Strong for its size, it has no hinged gate that can accidentally open under stress.

manteling: a climbing technique in which one moves up high enough to push down on a ledge with both hands until the body is supported on stiffened arms. The caver then replaces one hand with a high-stepping foot and moves up to stand on the ledge.

marble: a form of limestone metamorphosed by heat and pressure.

moon milk: whitish, puttylike form of flowstone that forms on an organic matrix.

natural anchor: a tree, boulder, or other natural feature that is well placed and strong enough to make a good anchor.

nut: an artificial chockstone, usually made of aluminum alloy and threaded with nylon cord. Nuts are fitted into cracks in the rock and usually can be used in place of pitons, which can scar the rock. A caver using only nuts needs no hammer, since nuts can be lifted out of their placements.

objective dangers: hazards that are not the result of flaws in a caver's equipment or technique. They include rockfall and tight crawlways.

onyx: a banded flowstone; travertine; calcite.

overhang: rock that exceeds 90 degrees.

pahoehoe: lava with smooth or billowy texture in which lava tubes may be found. (Contrasted with *aa*.)

palming: a friction hold in which a caver presses the palm of the hand into the rock.

pendulum: a sideways movement across a rock face by swinging on a rope suspended from above.

Petzl: a French manufacturer of climbing and caving equipment.

phreatic: below the water table. Most cave passages form this way and are characterized by rounded, tubular shapes. (Contrasted with *vadose*.)

pinch-out: a passage that becomes too narrow for a caver to squeeze through.

pit: a vertical or near-vertical drop requiring a rope to negotiate.

pit cave: a cave that must be entered through a pit, usually requiring vertical techniques to descend and ascend. Many caves have pit entrances created by breakdown, dome pit solution, or stream erosion.

piton: a metal wedge hammered into a crack until it is secure, used as an anchor point for protection or aid. One end has an eye into which a carabiner is clipped. In the United States, pitons are used only when absolutely necessary, because repeated use damages rock.

pooling: a method of rope management in which the climber places one end of the rope on the ground and piles concentric loops of rope on top.

protection: the anchors—such as chocks, bolts, or pitons—to which a climber connects the rope while ascending.

protection system: the configuration of anchors, runners, carabiners, ropes, harnesses, and belayer that combine to stop someone falling.

prusik: a technique for climbing a rope, originally by use of a prusik knot, now also by means of mechanical ascenders. The knot, invented by Karl Prusik in 1931, uses a loop of thin rope wound around a larger-diameter rope in such a way that the knot will slide freely when unweighted but will grip tightly to the main rope when a caver's weight is applied to it.

quadrangle: a U.S. Geologic Survey topographic map.

rappel: to descend by sliding down a rope. Friction for controlling the descent is provided by wraps of rope around the body or by a mechanical rappel device. The rope is usually doubled so that it can be pulled down afterward.

rappel device: see *descender.*

rappel point: the anchor for a rappel—that is, what the rope, or the sling holding it, is fastened to at the top.

rappel rack: a long, U-shaped steel bar that holds several brake bars and is used for rappelling.

rat tail: an excessively worn, unsafe climbing rope.

resurgence: a cave entrance from which water emerges.

rimstone dam: a wall-shaped calcite deposit that impounds, or formerly impounded, pools of water.

roof: an overhanging section of rock that is close to horizontal. Roofs vary in size from an eave of a few centimeters to giant cantilevers several yards wide.

rope: important element of the belay system. Modern climbing ropes are nylon kernmantle, usually 10 to 12 millimeters in diameter. According to John Forrest Gregory in *Rock Sport,* the ideal climbing rope would have all the following qualities: low impact force, low elongation under both impact force and low load, good handling qualities, light weight, water resistance, high ratings for holding falls, resistance to cutting and abrasion, and low price.

roping up: the act of a party of cavers tying themselves together with climbing ropes.

runner: a short length of nylon webbing or accessory cord tied or stitched to form a loop; used for connecting anchors to the rope and for other applications. Also called a *sling.*

runout: a section of a climb that is unprotectable, other than with bolts (which may be discouraged).

safety margin: the amount of extra strength built into climbing gear. For example, a carabiner may have a strength rating of 6,000 pounds, but it rarely has to support more than 3,000 pounds. Thus it has a cushion, or safety margin, of 3,000 pounds.

scale: the proportion between map distance and real distance. On a 1:10,000-scale map, for example, one unit on the map equals 10,000 of those same units on the ground.

scramble: an easy climb, usually without a rope. (Contrasted with *technical climbing*.)

scree: a long slope of loose stones on or below a hillside.

sea cave: a void or cavity in rock along a shore, caused by wave action along a zone of weakness, such as a fault or bedding plane.

seat harness: a harness usually made of 2-inch webbing with a waistband and separate leg loops, used for rappelling, prusiking, and belays.

self-belay: the technique of protecting oneself during a roped solo climb, often with a self-belay device.

shaft: a vertical cave passage; a pit.

show cave: a cave open to the public, usually with modifications, such as trails or steps. Also called a *commercial cave.*

single rope technique (SRT): a method of descending and ascending a single fixed rope.

sinkhole: a depression in the ground caused by solution of the underlying rock or by the collapse of the roof of an underlying cavern. These may be steep-sided or large, shallow depressions.

sinking stream: a stream that disappears underground. Also called an *insurgence.* See *swallow hole.*

sit bag: a cloth seat that cavers attach to the rock and sit in to make hanging from a wall more comfortable.

skylight: a hole in the ceiling of a cave, typically formed by ceiling collapse in a lava tube.

sling: see *runner.*

slope: the gradient of a rise or fall, or how much it deviates from the horizontal.

snap-link: a carabiner with a spring-loaded gate that opens inward. (Contrasted with *locking carabiner.*)

soda straw: a thin, hollow stalactite resembling a sipping straw. Its growth at the tip is due to water flowing down the inside of the straw. All stalactites begin this way.

soloing: climbing alone, whether roped or unroped, aided or free.

solution tube: a tubular-shaped passage created by dissolving action.

speleogen: a nondepositional cave feature, such as a ceiling pocket or scallop, that is produced by erosion or corrosion of bedrock.

speleogenesis: the process by which caves are formed.

speleology: the study of caves, encompassing their geology, geography, biology, history, and hydrology.

speleothem: a secondary mineral deposit, such as a stalactite or stalagmite, that forms in a cave.

spelunker: the noncaver's term for a caver. It fell out of favor with cavers when it was adopted by the media to describe all manner of people who go into caves.

spike: a finger of rock.

spongework: on cave walls, a complex system of tiny holes, tubes, and interconnected cavities that resembles Swiss cheese.

sprain: an injury that damages a ligament or ligaments, as well as joint capsules. In a severe sprain, one or more ligaments may be completely torn.

squeeze: a very tight passageway.

stalactite: a cylindrical or conical speleothem hanging from a ceiling or ledge.

stalagmite: a cylindrical or conical speleothem rising from a floor or ledge.

stemming: see *bridging*.

suck hole: a small swallow hole in a streambed that pirates water from the stream.

sump: a cave passage filled with water right to the roof.

swallet: see *swallow hole*.

swallow hole: a depression, seemingly closed, into which a stream disappears underground. Also called *swallet*.

talus: a sloping mass of rock, dirt, and debris at the base of a drop; a pile of jumbled rocks.

technical climbing: climbing that requires hardware, harnesses, ropes, and specialized boots. (Contrasted with *scramble*.)

toe-hooking: a climbing technique in which a toe is hooked around a rock edge.

topographic (topo) map: a map that uses contour lines, which connect points of equal elevation, to show the shape of the land, or topography.

traverse: to proceed around rather than straight over an obstacle; to climb from side to side. A traverse may be an easy walk along a ledge or a daunting passage. Protecting traverses is often difficult, because a fall will cause the caver to pendulum, ending up off route even if no injuries occur.

travertine: crystalline calcite.

troglobite: an animal that is fully adapted to life in total darkness and can only live underground.

troglophile: an animal species that may live underground but may also be found on the surface.

trogloxene: an animal, such as a bat, that visits caves for part of its activities but does not use the cave as a food source.

twilight zone: the area of a cave located between the entrance zone and the dark zone. It is sheltered from direct sunlight and has a more moderate environment than its neighbor zones. It is home to a large, diverse population of animals, including salamanders, bats, and, during severe winters, bears. Some animals hibernate in the twilight zone, but most exit to feed.

unidirectional anchor: an anchor that will hold securely if loaded from one direction but will pull free if loaded from any other direction.

vadose: said of caves formed by erosion above the water table, often tall canyons or rifts. (Contrasted with *phreatic*.)

vertical caving: caving that demands descending and ascending by rope.

virgin passage: a cave passage, or entire cave, previously undiscovered.

waist belay: a method of taking in and paying out a belayed active rope. The belayer passes the rope around his waist; the hand on the active rope side is the directing hand, and the hand on the slack rope side is the braking hand. Also called the *hip belay* or *body belay*.

water knot: the recommended knot for tying webbing into a loop.

water table: the highest level of ground water in a given area. Below this level, cave passages may be flooded.

webbing: flat or tubular nylon strapping.

weight training: lifting barbells and dumbbells to increase strength and correct muscular imbalances.

wild cave: an undeveloped cave in its natural state, in contrast to a commercial cave where lighting and paths have been added.

windchill: the cooling of the body that results from wind passing over its surface—especially dramatic if the surface is wet. It is a more useful measurement of meteorological discomfort than is temperature alone.

RESOURCES

The National Speleological Society, located in Huntsville, Alabama, is dedicated to the exploration, study, and conservation of caves. The organization, founded in 1941, brings together scientists, sport cavers, and conservationists, all of whom share a common interest in caves.

Here are some of the diverse services the National Speleological Society (NSS) provides its members:

- NSS Office. The national office performs various membership services, such as administering new memberships, address changes, renewals, and address labels. The office staffers operate a bookstore, sending out literature on caves around the world. They also create an annual, updated membership list, complete with addresses and telephone numbers, which is sent to all members. As of May 1, 1996, membership dues were as follows: Regular $25, Family $30, Associate $18.
- *NSS News.* This is a monthly magazine containing caving photos and articles, book reviews, analyses of new caving equipment, accident reports and safety tips, conservation concerns, and news about regional and national cavers and caving activities.
- *NSS Bulletin.* Published semiannually, this is the only national journal devoted to publishing scientific articles related to caves.
- Bookstore. Books, videos, and other caving items are available from the bookstore. NSS membership entitles you to a discount on most items.
- Library. A large collection of books and other publications devoted to speleology is located at the NSS office for use by members.
- Special Publications. The NSS promotes publications related to caves and coordinates with authors to ensure inclusion of NSS safety and conservation messages.
- *Speleo Digest.* This is an annual collection of the best articles, cartoons, and poems about caves culled from local organizations' newsletters.

- Audio-Visual Library. A lending library of slide programs and films on a wide variety of caving subjects is maintained for use by NSS members and other groups.
- Cave Files. The NSS is in the process of organizing all the available data on individual caves, including maps, articles, and research studies. This information is available to NSS members.
- Equipment. Various specialized equipment—caving, mapping, research—is available for lending to members conducting projects.
- Museum of Speleology. A collection of equipment and other items of historical interest.
- Photo Archives. The NSS maintains a central repository of historical photos.
- NSS-Owned Caves. The NSS owns several cave properties that are open to members.
- Research. The NSS uses grant money to promote the scientific study of caves. Grants are available to qualifying students and groups.
- Conservation Committee. The conservation committee organizes task forces in specific categories of cave destruction. It strives to educate the public on the importance of bats in the ecosystem. It also works with government agencies to stop cave vandalism, pass laws to protect caves, and promote new ideas, such as underground wilderness areas.
- National Cave Rescue Committee. A nationwide network of cavers, trained to handle the unique problems associated with underground accidents, is available to help those in need. In a cave-rescue emergency, call (800) 851-3051.
- Safety Committee. A committee analyzes new equipment and determines if, when, and how it should be used. It reports to members through the *NSS News* and at the national convention.
- Legal Committee. This committee provides legal advice on matters such as personal liability for caving accidents and grotto incorporation.
- Conventions. An annual convention is held that offers scientific symposia, vertical training, contests, photographic programs, and the chance to meet other cavers from around the country. You will also see the following:
  Cave-Mapping Salon. A display of the best cave maps, promoting quality, accuracy, and detail.

Photo Salon. A display of the best cave photography. Awards are given in several categories for quality and experimentation. *Cave Ballad Contest.* A contest for cave songs in several categories. Many of the past winners have been made into records.

Besides the benefits mentioned above, membership in the NSS affords you the opportunity to meet kindred spirits. Some cavers have traveled around the country, society list in hand, targeting spots where cavers live. Many will invite you to a meeting or on a cave trip, or offer you a place to stay.

GROTTOS

As of this writing, there are almost two hundred local chapters, or grottos, under the NSS umbrella. The number of active chartered NSS grottos continues to grow every year.

Members of grottos survey caves, install and maintain cave registers, build and maintain cave gates when necessary, and manage cave cleanup campaigns. Most grottos hold regular meetings and publish a newsletter. They maintain caver-training programs and stay up-to-date on the latest developments in equipment, safety, and technique. Grottos are often involved in cave conservation. Some grottos maintain libraries and equipment stores.

Although NSS members are not required to join grottos, they are urged to do so, for grottos are truly the backbone of the NSS. Membership in the NSS is more rewarding if you become active with other responsible cavers. Even if the members of your local grotto do nothing but cave together, they at least provide fellowship and responsible cavers from whom newcomers can learn.

According to writer, caver, and caving instructor David McClurg, organized caving clubs offer five things you can't provide yourself:

- They know how to cave and can show you how. Whether they have a formal training program or just start you off with easy caves, this is the way to learn. By asking questions and following what they do, you can learn the basics much more safely than you can alone or with other inexperienced cavers.
- They know where the caves are. This alone is worth the price of admission. New cavers inevitably learn that the best way—and sometimes the only way—to find a cave is to go there with someone who's been there before.
- They have specialized gear. This is the reason some groups

formed in the first place—to share and save money on expensive equipment. Some clubs pass the hard hat every meeting to save up for new equipment.

- They go caving. Most have regularly scheduled trips, some to horizontal caves, others to vertical caves. Many clubs print out the whole year's schedule in January. This lets them take full advantage of holidays and three-day weekends.

- They will usually welcome you, especially if you show a genuine interest in the sport. Some clubs have a designated greeter who watches for new people and gets them signed up. One caveat: Don't start out asking for a complete list of local caves. Many cavers are protective of their local caves.

You can obtain information about forming a new NSS grotto from the chairman of the NSS Internal Organizations Committee. You need a minimum of five NSS members to qualify for grotto status.

For more information about local and regional grottos, contact the National Speleological Society, 2813 Cave Ave., Huntsville, AL 35810, telephone (205) 852-1300, fax (205) 851-9241.

OTHER ORGANIZATIONS

The following organizations and agencies can also provide information on caves:

The National Outdoor Leadership School
P.O. Box AA
Lander, WY 82520
(800) 332-4100

Department of the Interior
Bureau of Land Management
1849 C Street, N.W.
Washington, DC 20240

Department of the Interior
National Park Service
1849 C Street, N.W.
P.O. Box 37127
Washington, DC 20013-7127

Department of Agriculture
U.S. Forest Service
Room 913-RPE
P.O. Box 96090
Washington, DC 20090-6090

SOURCES OF EQUIPMENT AND SUPPLIES

You can get a lot of your beginning caving equipment at an army-navy surplus store. It's a good source for camping equipment, cave packs, backup lights, and other assorted items of use to cavers. Inexpensive clothing for caving can be found at secondhand stores such as those run by Goodwill and the Salvation Army.

For more specialized gear, such as hard hats, carbide lamps, and most vertical equipment, the following caving suppliers are a better bet. Most of them will send you a catalog upon request.

Adventure 92
3661 Annelle Rd.
Murfreesboro, TN 37130
(615) 890-3948
caving and climbing equipment

Blue Water Ltd.
209 Lovvorn Rd.
Carrollton, GA 30117
caving rope and vertical equipment

Bob & Bob
P.O. Box 441
Lewisburg, WV 24901
(304) 772-5049
(304) 772-3074
caving and climbing equipment and books

Cave Books
5222 Eastland Dr.
New Carlisle, OH 45344
caving books and publications of the Cave Research Foundation

Custom Cave Gear
P.O. Box 7351
Charlottesville, VA 22906
vertical cave gear

Doug Feakes
RR 1, Box 118C
Falcon, MO 65470
(417) 668-7724
fine caving jewelry

Gibbs Products
2608 East 3820 South
Salt Lake City, UT 84109
(801) 272-8354
ascenders

Inner Mountain Outfitters
102 Travis Circle
Seaford, VA 23696-2412
(804) 898-2809
caving, climbing, and rescue equipment

NSS Bookstore
2813 Cave Ave.
Huntsville, AL 35810-4421
(205) 852-1300
fax: (205) 851-9241
caving books and novelties; discount to NSS members

Outdoor Ventures
Myer Distributing
73 E. Epler Ave.
Indianapolis, IN 46227
(317) 784-1255
military surplus, caving and camping equipment, and topo maps

PMI
P.O. Box 803
Lafayette, GA 30728
(800) 282-7673
caving ropes, rescue supplies, vertical gear, and Petzl gear

Speleobooks
Emily Davis Mobley
P.O. Box 10
Schoharie, NY 12157
(518) 295-7978
cave and bat books, prints, and ephemera

The Speleoshoppe
Ian Ellis
P.O. Box 297
Fairdale, KY 40118
(502) 367-6292
orders: (800) 626-5877
caving and climbing equipment and books

SSP Wilderness
P.O. Box 36
Petaluma, CA 94953
(800) 772-5948
camping and climbing equipment

U.S. Geological Survey
Distribution Branch
Building 41
Box 25286 Federal Center
Denver, CO 80225
topographical and geological maps and reports